Macmillan/McGraw-Hill Science

CHANGING EARTH

AUTHORS

Mary Atwater
The University of Georgia

Prentice Baptiste
University of Houston

Lucy Daniel
Rutherford County Schools

Jay Hackett
University of Northern Colorado

Richard Moyer
University of Michigan, Dearborn

Carol Takemoto
Los Angeles Unified School District

Nancy Wilson
Sacramento Unified School District

D1307526

The Sahara

Macmillan/McGraw-Hill School Publishing Company
New York   Chicago   Columbus

MACMILLAN / McGRAW-HILL

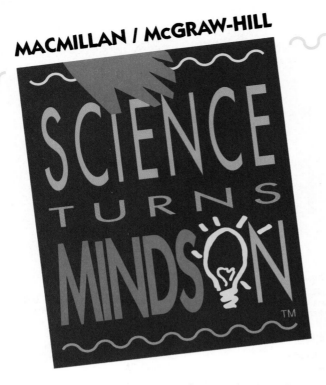

SCIENCE TURNS MINDS ON™

CONSULTANTS

Assessment:

Janice M. Camplin
Curriculum Coordinator, Elementary Science
Mentor, Western New York
Lake Shore Central Schools
Angola, NY

Mary Hamm
Associate Professor
Department of Elementary Education
San Francisco State University
San Francisco, CA

Cognitive Development:

Dr. Elisabeth Charron
Assistant Professor of Science Education
Montana State University
Bozeman, MT

Sue Teele
Director of Education Extension
University of California, Riverside
Riverside, CA

Cooperative Learning:

Harold Pratt
Executive Director of Curriculum
Jefferson County Public Schools
Golden, CO

Earth Science:

Thomas A. Davies
Research Scientist
The University of Texas
Austin, TX

David G. Futch
Associate Professor of Biology
San Diego State University
San Diego, CA

Dr. Shadia Rifai Habbal
Harvard-Smithsonian Center for Astrophysics
Cambridge, MA

Tom Murphree, Ph.D.
Global Systems Studies
Monterey, CA

Suzanne O'Connell
Assistant Professor
Wesleyan University
Middletown, CT

Environmental Education:

Cheryl Charles, Ph.D.
Executive Director
Project Wild
Boulder, CO

Gifted:

Sandra N. Kaplan
Associate Director, National/State Leadership
Training Institute on the Gifted/Talented
Ventura County Superintendent of Schools Office
Northridge, CA

Global Education:

M. Eugene Gilliom
Professor of Social Studies and Global Education
The Ohio State University
Columbus, OH

Merry M. Merryfield
Assistant Professor of Social Studies and Global
Education
The Ohio State University
Columbus, OH

Intermediate Specialist

Sharon L. Strating
Missouri State Teacher of the Year
Northwest Missouri State University
Marysville, MO

Life Science:

Carl D. Barrentine
Associate Professor of Biology
California State University
Bakersfield, CA

V.L. Holland
Professor and Chair, Biological Sciences
Department
California Polytechnic State University
San Luis Obispo, CA

Donald C. Lisowy
Education Specialist
New York, NY

Dan B. Walker
Associate Dean for Science Education and
Professor of Biology
San Jose State University
San Jose, CA

Literature:

Dr. Donna E. Norton
Texas A&M University
College Station, TX

Tina Thoburn, Ed.D.
President
Thoburn Educational Enterprises, Inc.
Ligonier, PA

Macmillan/McGraw-Hill School Division
10 Union Square East
New York, New York 10003

Printed in the United States of America

ISBN 0-02-274273-5 / 5

7 8 9 VHJ 99 98 97 96 95 94

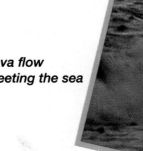

*Lava flow
meeting the sea*

Mathematics:

Martin L. Johnson
Professor, Mathematics Education
University of Maryland at College Park
College Park, MD

Physical Science:

Max Diem, Ph.D.
Professor of Chemistry
City University of New York, Hunter College
New York, NY

Gretchen M. Gillis
Geologist
Maxus Exploration Company
Dallas, TX

Wendell H. Potter
Associate Professor of Physics
Department of Physics
University of California, Davis
Davis, CA

Claudia K. Viehland
Educational Consultant, Chemist
Sigma Chemical Company
St. Louis, MO

Reading:

Jean Wallace Gillet
Reading Teacher
Charlottesville Public Schools
Charlottesville, VA

Charles Temple, Ph.D.
Associate Professor of Education
Hobart and William Smith Colleges
Geneva, NY

Safety:

Janice Sutkus
Program Manager: Education
National Safety Council
Chicago, IL

Science Technology and Society (STS):

William C. Kyle, Jr.
Director, School Mathematics and Science Center
Purdue University
West Lafayette, IN

Social Studies:

Mary A. McFarland
Instructional Coordinator of
Social Studies, K-12, and
Director of Staff Development
Parkway School District
St. Louis, MO

Students Acquiring English:

Mrs. Bronwyn G. Frederick, M.A.
Bilingual Teacher
Pomona Unified School District
Pomona, CA

Misconceptions:

Dr. Charles W. Anderson
Michigan State University
East Lansing, MI

Dr. Edward L. Smith
Michigan State University
East Lansing, MI

Multicultural:

Bernard L. Charles
Senior Vice President
Quality Education for Minorities Network
Washington, DC

Cheryl Willis Hudson
Graphic Designer and Publishing Consultant
Part Owner and Publisher, Just Us Books, Inc.
Orange, NJ

Paul B. Janeczko
Poet
Hebron, MA

James R. Murphy
Math Teacher
La Guardia High School
New York, NY

Ramon L. Santiago
Professor of Education and Director of ESL
Lehman College, City University of New York
Bronx, NY

Clifford E. Trafzer
Professor and Chair, Ethnic Studies
University of California, Riverside
Riverside, CA

STUDENT ACTIVITY TESTERS

Jennifer Kildow
Brooke Straub
Cassie Zistl
Betsy McKeown
Seth McLaughlin
Max Berry
Wayne Henderson

FIELD TEST TEACHERS

Sharon Ervin
San Pablo Elementary School
Jacksonville, FL

Michelle Gallaway
Indianapolis Public School #44
Indianapolis, IN

Kathryn Gallman
#7 School
Rochester, NY

Karla McBride
#44 School
Rochester, NY

Diane Pease
Leopold Elementary
Madison, WI

Kathy Perez
Martin Luther King Elementary
Jacksonville, FL

Ralph Stamler
Thoreau School
Madison, WI

Joanne Stern
Hilltop Elementary School
Glen Burnie, MD

Janet Young
Indianapolis Public School #90
Indianapolis, IN

CONTRIBUTING WRITERS

Mary Dylewski
Fred Schroyer

Changing Earth

Activities!

Features

Links

Departments

Changing Earth

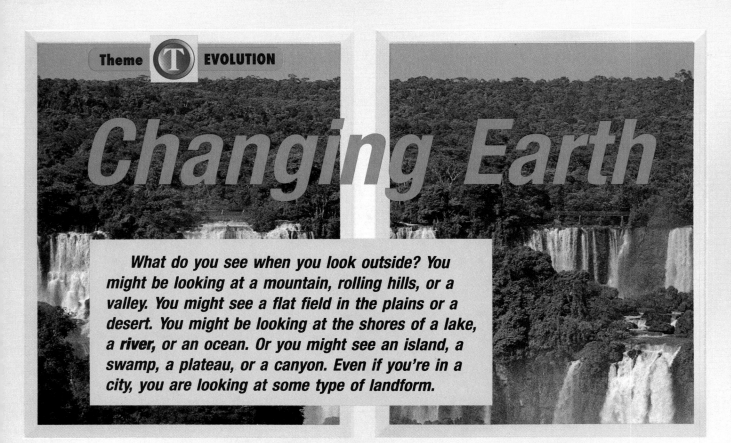

What do you see when you look outside? You might be looking at a mountain, rolling hills, or a valley. You might see a flat field in the plains or a desert. You might be looking at the shores of a lake, a **river**, or an ocean. Or you might see an island, a swamp, a plateau, or a canyon. Even if you're in a city, you are looking at some type of landform.

Iguacu Falls in Brazil

Although 71 percent of Earth's surface is water, most people live on land. You live on one type of landform, but you may have lived near or visited other types. For example, you may live in a city near an ocean. But you may have gone to a lake in the mountains for vacation. Maybe you have family or friends who live on other types of landforms.

Minds On! In your *Activity Log* on page 1, draw pictures of the different types of landforms you have visited. Label each landform. Compare your list with those of your classmates. ●

What Are the Types of Landforms?

Landforms are surface features. There are three general types of landforms—plains, plateaus, and mountains. These landforms are part of the 28 percent of Earth that is land. You may not visit most of the landforms on Earth. But you can see pictures of them and get a sense of what it would be like to be there.

Rocks are made of one or more minerals. **Minerals** are naturally-occurring, nonliving solids with certain physical structures and chemical properties.

Plateaus are uplifted high, flat regions, like the Massada Rock in Asia.

Mountains, like the Matterhorn, in Zermatt, Switzerland, are features that are higher than the surrounding land. Have you been to any of these kinds of areas?

Plains are large, flat areas of land like the Serengeti Plains in Africa.

The Sahara in Africa

Social Studies Link

Mountains on Earth

In your **Activity Log** on page 2, write the names of three mountains or mountain ranges in the United States. Then, write the names of two ranges or peaks not in the U.S. Now, find them on a map or globe. Compare your lists with those of your classmates.

8

Minds On! Sit quietly. Look around your room. Then close your eyes and count to 100 silently. Open your eyes. What changes do you observe? ●

Change is one thing we can count on. Although it may seem that Earth is the same every day, our planet never stands still! It revolves around the sun once a year. It rotates once every 24 hours, causing day and night. Much of Earth goes through seasonal changes every three months or so.

When you look outside, do you think that what you see has always been there? Have things changed much in your lifetime?

The skyline of Seattle, Washington, has changed since the early 1900s, but the mountains are basically the same.

As you look outside, can you imagine a dinosaur walking by? Can you imagine everything being covered by a shallow sea or swampland or ice?

Evidence indicates that what you see today hasn't always been the same. But major changes haven't happened in your lifetime, or in your grandparents' or great-grandparents' lifetimes. Major Earth changes happen over many, many, many years. When we talk about the time major Earth changes take to happen, we are talking about millions of years. Scientists estimate that Earth is 4.6 billion years old. They have organized the history of Earth into the **geologic** (jē´ ə loj´ ik) **time scale.**

In order to learn how to read Earth's history, you study earth science. Another name for it is **geology** (jē ol´ ə jē), which means "knowledge of Earth." **Geologists** (jē ol´ ə jists) are scientists who study Earth and its changes. They are detectives, collecting evidence to figure out what Earth was like in the past and how it works today.

Math 🔗 Link

Geologic Time

To get a sense of how old 4.6 billion years is, try to think in terms of seconds. How many seconds are there in a day? How many seconds are there in a year? How many years would it take to count 4.6 billion seconds? Earth is very old!

To find out how Earth has changed through time, you have to study Earth itself. Earth is the world's largest history book! Its rocks and landforms are like pages filled with clues about Earth processes and changes over time.

Mt. Kenya, Kenya in Africa

Language Arts Link

What Is Geology?

Geology is the study of Earth. *Geologists* study Earth. And *geologic time* is Earth's history, which began long before people existed. In your ***Activity Log*** on page 3, write what you think the word part *geo* and the word part *log* mean. Use a dictionary to check your answers. Then write two other words that have *geo* in them, and write two other words that have *log* in them. Are they related in meaning to *geology*?

Through the years of geologic time, many things happened on Earth that we will never know about. But using the evidence we have, people have been able to distinguish different parts of geologic time. In this unit you will get a chance to explore each of these parts. As you do, keep thinking about what you see around you. Think about how it might have been different at different times in Earth's history. See if you can understand more about why Earth is like it is and how it got to be this way.

To start thinking about how Earth has changed, set up this smelly activity and watch what happens over the next few weeks.

TRY THIS Activity!

Smelly Coal

Coal forms over long periods of geologic time. You can get an idea of how coal forms in this activity.

What You Need
container, sand, fern fronds, twigs, plant leaves, Activity Log page 4

In 2 weeks, you will need fine dirt and sand.

Pour water into the container until it measures 15 cm deep. Spread about 5 cm of fine sand on the bottom. Drop the leaves, fern fronds, and twigs into the container. Predict what will happen to the materials. Write your prediction in your *Activity Log.* Put the container out of the way of your nose. Leave it alone for 2 weeks.

Looking Ahead
You'll return to observe your container in Lessons 3 and 4 to see how coal forms and how fossils are made.

Ice Sheet Projects

Greenland Ice Sheet Project or GISP II is one that focuses on the history of Earth's environment. Its mission is to reveal changes in climate over the last 200 thousand years. These changes are recorded in a core of ice being drilled out of the polar ice sheets in Greenland.

Geologist involved with GISP II are using new drilling and analyzing techniques to reconstruct the changes in levels of gases in the air, precipitation, temperature, volcanic activity, humidity, and solar activity for the past 200 thousand years. This project will help us understand how our atmosphere has evolved and predict how it will continue to evolve.

Greenland is an ideal site for this study. In Greenland layers of ice have remained frozen for thousands of years. These ice layers collect and preserve the physical and chemical properties of Earth's atmosphere over time.

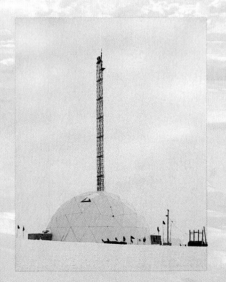

An earlier ice sheet project, GISP I, was completed in 1981. Over the course of seven years, scientists drilled a 10.2-centimeter (4-inch) diameter ice core to a depth of 2,037 meters (6,683 feet).

This ice core shows a history of Earth's climate that dates back 70 thousand years. That's about 1,000 times longer than any human is expected to live.

13

Science in Literature

There are lots of books that help to reveal the mysteries of Earth's history.

***Footprints in the Swamp* by Marie Halun Bloch**
New York: Atheneum, 1985

For 140 million years, dinosaurs roamed an Earth that was much different from the one you know today. When dinosaurs became extinct 65 million years ago, many smaller creatures survived. This book explores the life of one of these small animals, an ancestor of today's opossum. As you study Earth's history, read this book to get a picture of what life was like during the age of the dinosaurs. What was it really like for a small mammal-ancestor to live among the dinosaurs?

Footprints in the Swamp
by Marie Halun Bloch

Illustrated by Robert Shetterly

Dinosaurs Walked Here and Other Stories Fossils Tell by Patricia Lauber. New York: Bradbury Press, 1987.

Explore the fossil record found in Earth's crust. See for yourself evidence of plants and animals that lived in different eras of Earth's history. Wonderful pictures show you the evidence of ancient landforms. Like a detective, read this book for clues about what your state may have been like throughout geologic time.

Other Good Books To Read

Glaciers: Ice on the Move by Sally M. Walker. Minneapolis: Carolrhoda Books, Inc., 1990.

At some periods in Earth's history, ice covered major portions of the land. Glaciers that exist today help show how these rivers of ice may have carved some of Earth's landforms over time. Read this book to see how glacial movements may have changed the land where you live.

The Enormous Egg by Oliver Butterworth. Boston: Brown Books, 1956.

A *triceratops* was a kind of dinosaur that lived over 100 million years ago. What would happen if a triceratops hatched today? What would you do with it? Could it survive in present times? How would people react? Read about one boy's adventure when he discovers an enormous egg.

The Evolution Book by Sara Stein. New York: Workman Publishing Company, Inc., 1986.

Lots of pictures, interesting facts, and fun project ideas in this book will help you discover the secrets of Earth's history.

Volcano: The Eruption and Healing of Mount St. Helens by Patricia Lauber. New York: Bradbury Press, 1986.

Read this award-winning book to see how volcanoes could have shaped Earth's features from the beginning of its history.

The Work of Weathering

The Cenozoic Era
65 Million Years Ago to the Present

Neither snow, nor rain, nor heat, nor gloom of night stays these couriers from the swift completion of their appointed rounds.
New York City Post Office Inscription
Herodotus 485–425 B.C.

Although weather and climate may not keep mail carriers from working, they certainly do change the shape of Earth over time.

eathering and climate changes have caused valleys, lakes, and plains. Some of these changes occurred rapidly.

Other changes are slower and harder to see. These changes slowly happen underground in Earth's rocks and water. And Earth's climate may be changing today.

Minds On! What do you think would happen if Earth's average temperature got ten degrees colder? Would your life change any? What would happen if it got 30 degrees colder? What would happen if it got warmer? Write your predictions in your *Activity Log* on page 5. ●

Alps, Switzerland in Europe

Activity!

Moving Ice

What could happen if massive amounts of ice moved from one place to another? What if it carried rocks and soil with it? In this activity you'll observe how moving ice affects landforms.

What You Need

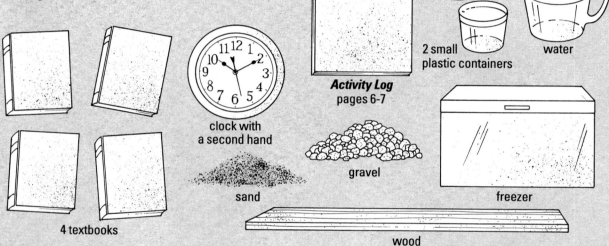

Activity Log
pages 6-7

2 small plastic containers

water

sand

gravel

freezer

clock with a second hand

4 textbooks

wood

What To Do

1 Pour water into the containers until they are half full.

2 Add sand and gravel to cover the bottom of 1 container.

3 Place both containers in a freezer until frozen.

4 Remove the containers and remove the blocks of ice from them. Let them stand for 10 min.

5 Lean the wood against the textbooks to make a slope.

6 Place the ice block without the sand and gravel at the top of the board. Time how long it takes for it to reach the bottom. Record the time in your *Activity Log.*

7 Place the block with the sand and gravel at the top of the board. Time and record how long it takes for this block to reach the bottom.

What Happened?

1. Which block took longer to go down the slope?
2. What happened to the wood as each block went down?

What Now?

1. If the blocks were heavier, would it make a difference in the length of time it takes them to go down?
2. How would a huge mass of ice move?
3. What would happen to landforms in the path of a huge, moving ice body?
4. What could the moving ice body leave behind?

EXPLORE

19

Ice on the Move

Rivers of ice, or **glaciers** (glā´ shərz), are massive bodies of ice. They flow slowly over land in cold polar regions and in high mountain valleys. You will have a sense of what glacial ice is like if you pour water on a snowball to make a ball of ice.

Glacial ice forms in the same way some metamorphic (met´ ə môr´ fik) rocks form. When rocks are subjected to changes in temperature and pressure, they can change from one form to another. Like metamorphic rocks, snow is changed into glacial ice through temperature and pressure.

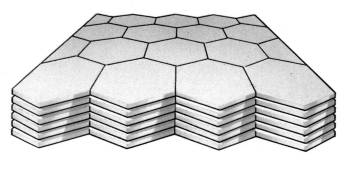

Layers of snow build up because winter snowfall is greater than summer melting.

The pressure of the layers of snow crushes the snow crystals and turns them into compacted ice particles.

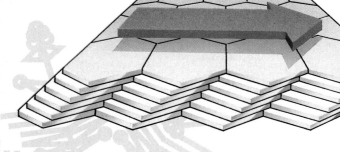

Ice crystals slide against each other causing a glacier to flow.

Huge amounts of ice can move with no outside help. Like in the Explore Activity on pages 18–19, ice moves due to gravity. The melting ice at the bottom of the glacier helps it slide down a valley. Masses of ice can also move when the mass presses against the rock below. This pressure makes the lower ice like dough, causing it to bend and flow. This also allows the ice to move slowly.

One type of glacier is a **continental glacier**. These are enormously thick layers of ice that cover huge areas of land. They are also called icecaps or ice sheets. Today these glaciers are found in Greenland and Antarctica.

Continental glacier of Antarctica

Activity!

Making Glacier Snow Cones

How do glaciers form?

What You Need
spoon, paper towel, ice shavings, powdered drink mix, small paper cup, Activity Log page 8

First write a hypothesis, or educated guess, in your **Activity Log** to explain what will happen if you press ice shavings together. Put a layer of ice shavings on the bottom of the cup. Sprinkle the drink mix over them with a spoon. Add another layer of ice shavings and another layer of drink mix. Fold the top of the cup inward to cover the ice. Now push down on the top of the folded cup as hard as you can. Keep pushing for at least 25 s. Cut one side of the cup apart to expose your layers of ice.

What happened to the ice shavings? Based on your observations, form a hypothesis to explain how glaciers turn layers of snow into rivers of ice. Write your hypothesis in your **Activity Log.** What happens to materials in air that are trapped in layers of snow?

Valley glaciers are long, narrow bodies of ice that fill high mountain valleys where snow builds up and presses down year after year. The Andes in South America, the Rockies in North America, the European Alps, and the Southern Alps in New Zealand all have valley glaciers. Because of steep mountain slopes, valley glaciers may move faster than continental glaciers. Valley glaciers in mountains near the equator occur at higher altitudes than in mountains in Alaska or Norway. Why do you think that is so?

Glaciers move at different speeds. Most move less than 30 centimeters (1 foot) a day. But some glaciers have moved more than 30 meters (100 feet) in one day.

Valley glacier

*A **moraine** (mə rān´) is the sediment left behind as hills or ridges when the glacier melts.*

*When glaciers reach the sea, huge chunks of ice fall into the sea. These chunks of ice are called **icebergs**.*

Big ice blocks may be left behind when glaciers begin to melt. In other places the glacier may erode parts of the land. Depressions may be left in the land when the glacier finally melts, and these can create lakes or small ponds.

Valley glaciers make ice-carved mountain ridges, U-shaped valleys, and sharp peaks out of mountain rock. Deeply eroded valleys are often the result of valley glacial activity.

All that ice can't move without making major changes in the landscape. When your model glacier moved down the wood plank, water may have run in front of it. Gravel or sand may have been left behind. Glaciers work in the same way, but on a much larger scale. The melting ice in front of the glacier deposits layers of sand and gravel. Rocks at the base of the glacier can scrape long grooves over the surface of rock on the valley floor.

Erratics (i rat´ iks) are rocks that glaciers have carried far from their original sources. Glaciers not only move broken rock, but they also create broken rock when they move.

23

Activity!

Dissolve a Rock

What happens when rain falls on certain landforms?

What You Need
vinegar, water, 2 pieces of limestone, 2 small containers, *Activity Log* page 9

Put a piece of limestone in each container. Predict what will happen if you pour vinegar (acid) over the limestone. Predict what will happen if you pour water over it. Write your predictions in your *Activity Log*. Pour vinegar over the limestone in one container. Pour water over the limestone in the other container to control your variables. Record your observations.

How can rain change rocks? How long do you think it would take rain to dissolve a rock? How would you know if a rock were being dissolved by rain?

Weathering Changes Earth

Along with glaciers, rain also affects the appearance of landforms. Heavy rain loosens rocks from mountains and hills. Some rocks can be worn down when certain chemicals mix with water. Do the activity to see how chemicals affect limestone.

The Grand Canyon

Wind, water, ice, and gravity also cause erosion. Erosion (i rō´zhən) is a process by which loose materials are transported and deposited somewhere else.

Think of the Explore Activity in which you slid the "glacier" with sand and rocks down the wood board. The "ice glacier" scraped away pieces of wood from the board.

Rain and wind also cause erosion. To clean the board off, you could have used a spray of water to wash the rocks and sand away. Or once it dried, you could have blown it clean with air. Erosion works in the same way. The soil in the Great Plains in the United States, for example, is being eroded by water. The soil is carried from the ground into rivers and streams.

Niagara Falls is midway along the Niagara River between Lake Ontario and Lake Erie.

Niagara Falls dates back to 10 thousand years ago. Then the falls were 11 kilometers (7 miles) further down the river than they are today. The pounding water has slowly worn away rocks, about 1 meter (3 feet) a year. In about 25 thousand years, Niagara Falls will disappear, reaching Lake Erie.

Math Link

No More Honeymooners

Calculate how far Niagara Falls has eroded since you were born. Subtract your birth year from this year. Multiply by how fast the falls are eroding. This is how many meters the falls have eroded in your lifetime. How far will they erode by the time you are 30 and by the time you are 65?

Changing Earth's Crust

What do all these processes do to Earth's thin layer of "skin," or **crust**, that covers the Earth? The crust under the ocean is about six kilometers (four miles) thick and is more dense than the crust that is under land.

The crustal changes we've talked about so far have taken place throughout geologic time, but most occurred during the Cenozoic Era. It is the most recent period of geologic time. During this time, glaciers, earthquakes, volcanoes, and climate changes have affected the planet.

But most changes have resulted from the many episodes of glacial activity. Today glaciers cover ten-and-a-half percent of Earth's land, but glaciers have advanced and melted many times throughout the Cenozoic Era.

Just 200 years ago, Glacier Bay National Park in Alaska was entirely covered by glacial ice. The retreating glaciers have exposed nearly 600 meters (2,000 feet) of land per year since then.

The Ice Ages

Glaciers occurred during periods of Earth's history called **ice ages**. Evidence of glacial activity in the past helps us figure out what the climate was like. Geologists know there have been several major ice ages, each lasting many thousands of years.

The most recent ice age in the Cenozoic Era began about 2 million years ago and ended about 10 thousand years ago. Average temperatures were 10–25 degrees colder than today. Ice covered 30 percent of Earth's land area. We know more about it than any other ice age, because evidence has been less disturbed by other crustal changes than evidence from earlier ice ages.

Minds On! Look at your *Activity Log* page 5 and find the predictions you made about the effects of lower average temperatures at the beginning of this lesson. Do you want to change any of your predictions? Write a hypothesis in your *Activity Log* on page 10 about one effect explaining why it would happen. ●

Landforms also formed during the Cenozoic Era as a result of glacial activity. In Kelleys Island, Ohio, glacial grooves in the rocks show some of the results of glacial movements.

Arizona's Grand Canyon shows us a great deal of geologic history. Exposed rock layers may date back more than 2 billion years.

Gathering Evidence of Geologic History

Knowledge about glaciers is very recent considering geologic time. In 1837, a 30-year-old Swiss scientist, Louis Agassiz (ä´ gə sē), presented the idea that glaciers had shaped many landforms. However, the scientists he told could not believe that there could have been so much ice covering the land or that it could have caused so much change. But slowly people changed their minds in the face of mounting evidence.

Evidence of change comes from core samples that show layers of rock that make up Earth's crust.

In the GISP II project, scientists will be analyzing ice core samples.

Evidence of geologic history can also be found in fossils. **Fossils** (fos´ əlz) are traces or remains of plants or animals. Studying fossils in rocks can tell you about the climate of a time in geologic history. Sometimes people find similar fossils in different areas in rock layers of the same age. This means that the climate of the two places was similar while these sediments were being laid down.

This is a site where fossils are being found that help scientists learn about Earth's history.

TRY THIS

Activity!

Core Sampling

See how people get evidence for their hypotheses about Earth's history.

What You Need
3 different kinds of bread, peanut butter, fruit spread, plastic knife, manicotti noodle, *Activity Log* **page 11**

Spread peanut butter on 1 piece of bread. Then, lay another piece of bread on top of it. Spread fruit spread on that piece of bread and cover it with the third piece of bread. Press the manicotti noodle against the top of the sandwich and twist into the layers. Carefully remove your core sample by cracking open the noodle to observe the layers. Describe it in your *Activity Log*. If you wish, you can eat your core sample.

How is core sampling valuable to the study of Earth's history? How else do you think people could see layers of Earth?

27

The word part *ceno* means "recent," and *zoic* means "animals." Geologic time is a division of the eras, or time periods, in which different types of animals lived.

The common name for the Cenozoic Era is "Age of Mammals." Mammals became the major land animals during this era. Fish, algae, and microscopic animals became the major ocean life. Flowering plants, mainly grasses, also dominated the era.

Nearly half of all mammals that came to be, also became extinct in the Cenozoic Era. This may be because when glacial ice melted, large groups of animals were stranded in places where there wasn't enough food. Secrets of the past are sometimes buried in the ice.

Today the saber-toothed cat, mastodon, long-horned bison, and mammoth are extinct.

In 1977, a 40 thousand-year-old woolly mammoth calf was uncovered frozen in the ice in Siberia.

Mammoth

Saber-toothed cat

Dinosaurs Walked Here and Other Stories Fossils Tell

Chapter two, "Gnats, Mammoths, and Saber-toothed Tigers," has pictures and information about many animals. Chapter three, "Layers of Fossils," tells you how scientists find evidence about climates in layers of rocks. After reading these chapters, in your *Activity Log* on page 12, write a plan for how you would begin to examine a 40 thousand-year-old animal. Who could help you? What precautions would you take? What would you want to find out about it?

Long-horned bison

Sum It Up

Like a complex machine, several different systems work together to change Earth. The weather system, the water cycle, and the rock cycle cause changes in Earth's landforms. Glaciers form as a result of changes in weather and climate.

Long periods of wet and cold weather result in ice ages in which large ice sheets and valley glaciers sculpt the surface. Plants and animals must adapt to these changing conditions to survive. We learn about Earth's past by studying its landforms and fossil records, and inferring what it might have been like long ago.

Platygonus

Critical Thinking

1. How is the formation of glaciers like the formation of metamorphic rock and the metamorphosis of butterflies and frogs? How is it different?

2. How could humans adapt to another ice age? What do you predict would happen to plants and animals?

3. What major change in life on Earth do you think will determine the end of the Cenozoic Era and the beginning of a new era?

Pieces of Crust

The Mesozoic Era
250 to 65 Million Years Ago

*If all the seas were one sea,
What a great sea that would be!*
Nursery Rhyme

North America

Africa

Asia

Antarctica

30

South America

Australia

Europe

What if all the seas were one sea? And all the continents were one continent? Climate is not the only force that has affected Earth's surface. People are just beginning to understand how movements of the Earth's crust and the layer below have shaped and reshaped Earth's landforms throughout its history.

D o you like jigsaw puzzles? How can you tell which pieces fit together? Do you look for shapes and patterns that match? From out in space, do Earth's continents look like pieces of a big jigsaw puzzle?

Minds On! Think of Earth's continents as a giant jigsaw puzzle. In your *Activity Log* on page 13, draw the continents as you think they might fit together. ●

Now get ready to make another model to discover how scientists are putting together the puzzle of Earth's continents. Think about how these models help solve part of the puzzle of Earth's history.

Activity!

Cruising With the Continents

You can see how continents might fit together. See if you can find an underlying structure to the Earth's crust and the layer below. How might this underlying structure have changed Earth over time?

world map

What You Need

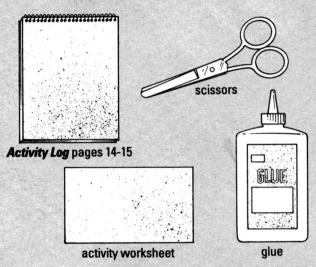

Activity Log pages 14-15

scissors

activity worksheet

glue

What To Do

1 Cut out each piece.

2 Arrange the pieces in your *Activity Log* to form a map of Earth.

3 Glue the pieces in place.

4 With a pencil, label the continents—Asia, South America, North America, Africa, Europe, Antarctica, and Australia.

5 Use the world map to sketch in the locations of the following landforms—the Cascade Mountains of North America, the Andes of South America, the Atlas Mountains of northern Africa, the Himalayas of Asia, and the Alps of Europe.

6 Make dots to show where any volcanoes you know of have erupted.

7 Make marks to show where any earthquakes you know of have occurred.

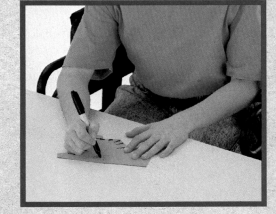

What Happened?

1. How many pieces did you have?
2. How many continents did you have?
3. Locate where you live on the map. What plate do you live on? Which continent do you live on?

What Now?

1. If each piece shows an actual piece of Earth's crust and the layer below, why do you think some earthquakes, volcanoes, and mountains occur where they do? Write your hypothesis in your *Activity Log.*
2. Do you think the pieces of crust and the layer below could move? If so, in which directions?
3. What do you think might happen if 2 pieces of crust and the layer below collided?
4. What do you think might happen if 2 pieces of crust and the layer below moved apart?
5. Do you think the continents could have been connected at one time? Why or why not?

EXPLORE

Mapping the Mesozoic Era

In the Explore Activity on pages 32–33, you moved pieces of Earth's crust to form a map of the planet. You saw that the continents are part of these pieces. But you may not have been able to see how the pieces could move. Or you may not have thought that they had moved many times throughout geologic time.

Remember that the Cenozoic Era started with colder climates that led to several ice ages. 250 to 65 million years ago, before the Cenozoic Era, was the Mesozoic Era. *Meso* means "middle." Lots of scientific evidence indicates that Earth's landmasses and oceans changed during the Mesozoic Era. At the start of the Mesozoic Era, studies show that all the continents we know of today were together in one huge landmass.

About 250 million years ago

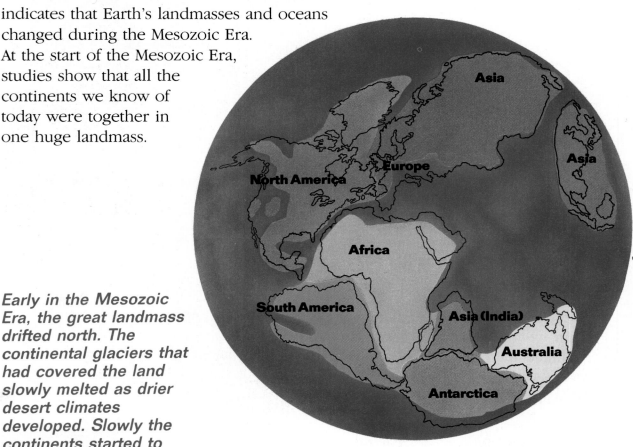

Early in the Mesozoic Era, the great landmass drifted north. The continental glaciers that had covered the land slowly melted as drier desert climates developed. Slowly the continents started to break apart.

North America split off from Africa. South America, Africa, India, and probably China moved to the equator. Australia and Antarctica stayed near the South Pole. The Atlantic and Indian oceans also began to form.

Minds On!

Locate the place in which you now live on the map of the early Mesozoic Era. How close is it to the equator? What do you think the climate would have been like at that time? ●

In the middle of the Mesozoic Era, the climate also began to change. It stayed warm, but became wetter as the rain watered the deserts. Eventually shallow seas formed over much of the land.

The Andes in South America began to form. North America moved west. As it did, 70 million years ago, the Rockies started to form.

About 70 million years ago

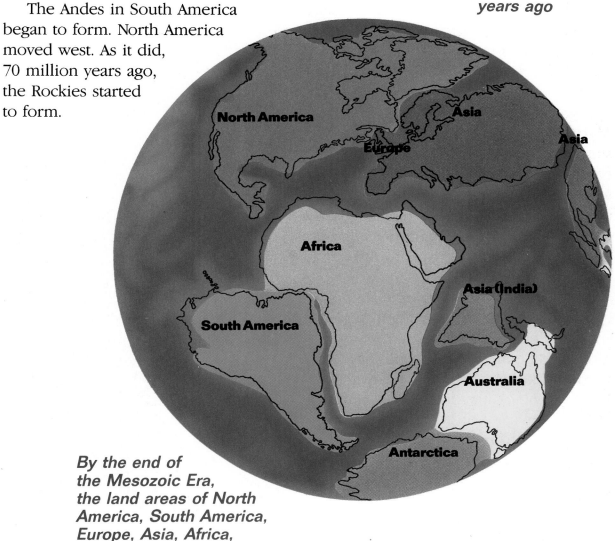

North America

Asia

Asia

Europe

Africa

Asia (India)

South America

Australia

Antarctica

By the end of the Mesozoic Era, the land areas of North America, South America, Europe, Asia, Africa, India, Australia, and Antarctica had all separated and began moving toward the positions they are in today.

Activity!

Mapping the Continents

You can show how the continents moved throughout the Mesozoic Era.

What You Need

paper, pencil, scissors, *Activity Log* page 16

Roughly trace or draw the continents as you drew them for the Minds On! on page 31. Label them. Then cut them out. Read through the descriptions of continental movements in the Mesozoic Era. Move your puzzle pieces to match what is being described.

During the Mesozoic Era, how do you think the climate changed where you live?

Continental Drift

For many years, most people thought Earth's continents had always been where they are now. It wasn't until the 20th century that Alfred Wegener (ve´ gən ûr), a German meteorologist, theorized that Earth's landmasses were once joined. His hypothesis was called **continental** (kon´ tə nen´ təl) **drift.**

Over millions of years, he claimed, the continents had moved into their present spots. He based his ideas on the way Africa and South America could fit together like puzzle pieces. He matched rocks on the continents to show similar climates. He also showed the similarity of fossils found on each continent. He said plants and animals could not possibly have been able to cross oceans to reach other continents.

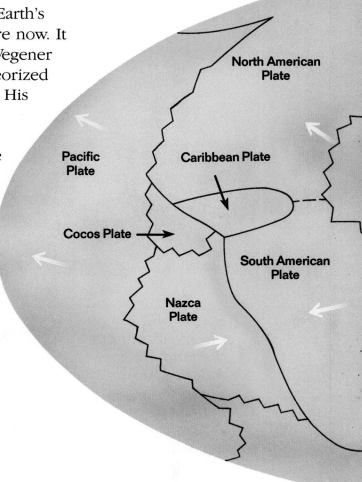

North American Plate

Pacific Plate

Caribbean Plate

Cocos Plate

South American Plate

Nazca Plate

Plate Tectonics

A **theory** (thē´ ə rē) is a carefully-built set of ideas based on evidence that explains many scientific observations. Wegener's hypothesis could not explain continental movement. But in the 1960s, a theory was developed based on continental drift that changed the way people thought about Earth's surface.

The **plate tectonics** (tek ton´ iks) theory states that it is the plates, not the continents themselves, that move. Plate tectonics explains how the continents move, and also how mountains are formed, and why some earthquakes and volcanic eruptions occur.

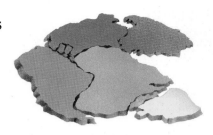

*When Wegener proposed his continental drift hypothesis, he claimed that at one time there was only one landmass. He called this **Pangaea** (pan jē´ə). He thought the continents had broken apart and moved.*

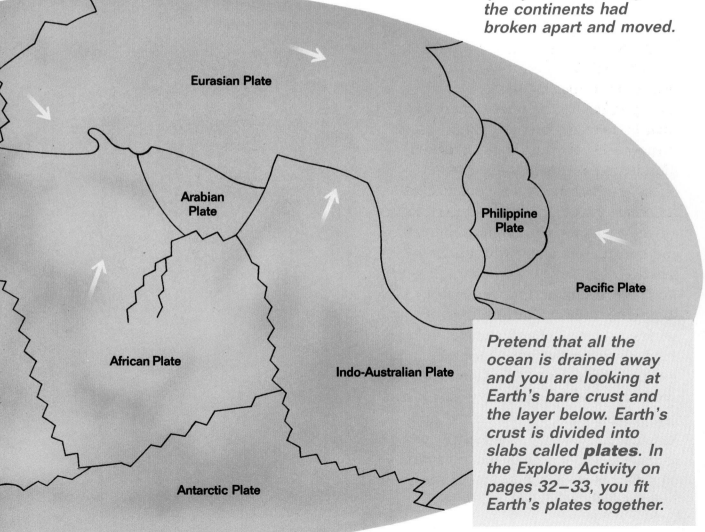

Eurasian Plate

Arabian Plate

Philippine Plate

Pacific Plate

African Plate

Indo-Australian Plate

Antarctic Plate

*Pretend that all the ocean is drained away and you are looking at Earth's bare crust and the layer below. Earth's crust is divided into slabs called **plates**. In the Explore Activity on pages 32–33, you fit Earth's plates together.*

Activity!

Breaking Up

What happened to Pangaea? Think about it as you try this.

What You Need

1 c flour, 1 tsp. salt, bowl, spoon, water, waxed paper, *Activity Log* page 17

Mix the flour, salt, and a little bit of water in the bowl until it is just moist enough to stay in a ball. Then knead the dough in the bowl. Press the mixture onto the waxed paper with your hands. Flatten it with your hands. Set the flattened dough in the sun (about 2 days) until the mixture dries completely.

Erode the "crustal plate" by pushing down on the outside edges until it cracks. Why do you think plates may have irregular shapes? What do you think could have happened to cause the crustal plates to break apart?

Plate Movements

Look back to the puzzle pieces in the Explore Activity on pages 32–33. How many plates did you count? Earth has nine large plates and a few smaller ones. Some of the plates contain only ocean crust and upper mantle, while others contain both continental crust and ocean crust along with upper mantle.

The breakup and movement of Pangaea is only the most recent of several cycles of plate movements in Earth's history. Evidence for earlier movements is hard to find. But evidence proves that there wasn't just one supercontinent that existed until it began to break up. Continents have formed, come together, moved apart, and disappeared in cycles over the life of Earth.

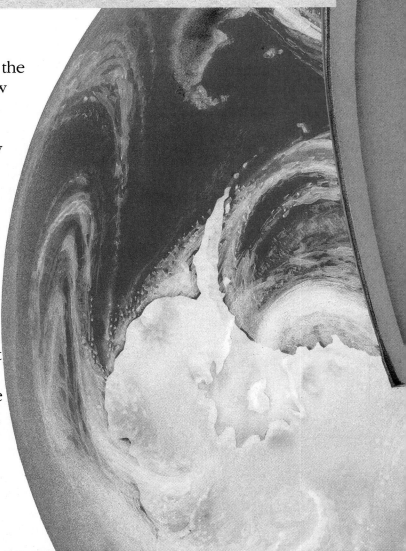

Oceanic Plate

Minds On! As the plates spread apart, they slowly widen the Atlantic Ocean about 2.5 centimeters (1 inch) each year. Remember that continents are riding on these plates. Are South America and Africa getting closer together or farther apart across the Atlantic Ocean? Are South America and Asia getting closer together or farther apart across the Pacific Ocean? ●

*Earth's **mantle** (man´ təl) is a layer of rocks 2,900 kilometers (1,800 miles) thick. The top of the mantle is partly fluid. It may be the currents in this fluid rock that make the plates move.*

The thickness of Earth's crust ranges from 6–70 kilometers (4–43 miles). Beneath the crust is the mantle.

Plates consist of Earth's crust and part of the upper layer of the mantle.

Continental Plate

Earth's plates are 75–120 kilometers (46.5–74.4 miles) thick.

Math 🔗 Link

Moving Plates

If a plate moves five centimeters (two inches) a year, how many kilometers would it move in one million years? How much would it move over the course of the Mesozoic Era, 185 million years? Do your calculations in your ***Activity Log*** on page 18.

Plate Boundaries

The arrows on the puzzle plates in the Explore Activity on pages 32–33, show the general directions the plates move. There are three ways plates interact.

They can move away from each other like the Nazca Plate and the Pacific Plate.

They can slide past each other like the Pacific Plate and the North American Plate.

They can collide like the African Plate and the Eurasian Plate.

TRY THIS Activity!

Collision Course

What happens when plates collide?

What You Need

2 phone books, *Activity Log* page 19

Take the phone books and place them so the pages are facing each other. Now push them together very slowly. Record your observations in your *Activity Log.*

If the phone books were plates, what landform would 2 colliding plates make?

Minds On! In your *Activity Log* on page 19, write predictions of what you think happens when two plates move apart. What happens when they slide past each other? Discuss your predictions with your classmates. ●

The highest point on Earth, Mount Everest at 8,848 meters (29,028 feet), is in the Himalayan Mountains. It is the result of the collision of two continental plates. This mountain range, formed during the Cenozoic Era, is only 40 million years old.

When two continental plates collide, mountains form. The Rocky Mountains and the Andes formed during the Mesozoic Era as a result of plate movements.

Minds On! Look back at your puzzle in your *Activity Log* on page 14. Name the plates that are involved in the formation of the Andes, Himalayas, Alps, Atlas, and Cascade Mountains. ●

SCIENCE TECHNOLOGY AND Society

Focus on Technology

Confirming Plate Tectonics

Technology has helped to confirm what happens underwater at plate boundaries. Deep-sea drilling has shown that the rocks under the oceans are much younger than most of the rocks on the continents.

By the early 1990's, scientists from around the world involved with the drilling program were drilling into the ocean floor. From core samples, scientists hope to better explain the movement of Earth's plates that causes rearrangement of the continents, earthquakes, and volcanoes.

Geologists use sonar to locate the drilling site and a remote TV camera to position the drill pipe. They will test the samples of crust for age, mineral content, and other characteristics.

Life in the Mesozoic Era

Another name for the Mesozoic Era is "Age of the Dinosaurs." *Dinosaur* means "terrible lizard." At the beginning of the Mesozoic Era, before the continents split apart, land animals could populate every part of the world simply by walking across the land. So, dinosaur fossils have been found around the globe. Although there were more insects than any other animal, the many species of dinosaurs were the dominant land-dwelling vertebrates on Earth.

Dinosaurs began dying out about 66 million years ago. Whatever happened during the end of the Mesozoic Era, dinosaurs didn't survive into the Cenozoic Era.

Tyrannosaurus rex

Hesperornis

Some dinosaurs were strictly carnivores, or meat-eaters, like Tyrannosaurus rex (ti ran´ ə sôr´ əs reks).

Flowering plants appeared near the end of the Mesozoic Era.

Literature ✍ Link

Footprints in the Swamp

Read *Footprints in the Swamp* by Marie Halun Bloch. As you read, choose your favorite dinosaur, mammal, and plant. In your **Activity Log** on page 20 draw and label them. Did the author give you the same picture of the life, climate, and landscape of the Mesozoic Era as this unit does?

Sum It Up

Right now there are seven continents, but these were once part of a single landmass called Pangaea. Over millions of years, this single landmass broke apart into separate plates that carried the continents on them. Slowly, they moved into their present positions. Many landforms, including ridges and trenches under the sea, and mountain ranges on land, resulted from the movement of the plates.

We know change has occurred, but we don't fully understand why or how these changes happened over millions of years. Our clues are in the ice and rocks of Earth.

Homalocephale

Critical Thinking

1. How would life on Earth today be different if there were only one large continent and one large ocean?
2. What do you think will happen to the position of the continents over the next 200 million years?
3. How is the Mesozoic Era different from the Cenozoic Era? How is it the same?

Deinosuchus

43

A Dash of Salt, A Lump of Coal

The Paleozoic Era
570 to 250 Million Years Ago

Some people think throwing a pinch of salt over their shoulders will bring good luck. The little bit of salt you might have thrown over your shoulder is left from the oceans of over 300 million years ago.

Bonneville Salt Flats, Utah

Salt is one of the most abundant minerals on Earth. It's in our food, our ocean water, and our blood, sweat, and tears. Saltiness is one of the four basic tastes. Salt is cheap to buy and plentiful, so taking it for granted is easy. We use salt to make paper, ice cream, soap, glass, plastics, dyes, medicines, and food preservatives. We use it to soften water and to lower the freezing temperature of water on highways. Its chemical name is sodium chloride (NaCl), and its mineral name is halite.

You could not live without salt. It controls the amount of water in your cells so they don't burst. It also helps conduct your body's electrical signals that make your muscles contract and your heart beat.

Where does this familiar compound come from? What could it and other Earth resources have to do with the 4.6 billion-year history of Earth?

Activity!

Salty Beds

How has salt collected on Earth? What clues can it give us about Earth's past climate and geology?

What You Need

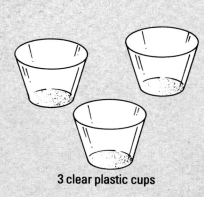

3 clear plastic cups

Activity Log pages 22-23

spoon

water

table salt

What To Do

1 Pour 12 tsp. water into each cup.

2 Mix 3 tsp. salt with the water in 1 cup. Mix 1 tsp. salt with the water in the second cup. Put no salt in the third cup. The different amounts of salt represent the variable that you are controlling in the activity.

3 Predict what will happen to the water and salt in each cup over several days. Write your predictions in your *Activity Log*.

4 Observe the cups each day until the water evaporates. Write any changes you see in your *Activity Log*.

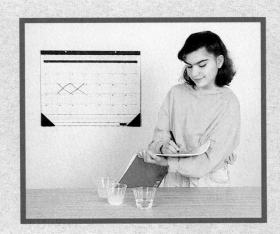

What Happened?

1. What remained in each cup after the water evaporated?
2. Did the salt affect the rate of evaporation of water in each cup?

What Now?

1. Describe how you think salt beds on Earth may have formed.
2. What could have happened to the water that helped form the salt beds?
3. If salt beds are found in Chicago, Illinois, what does that tell you about the geologic history of that area?
4. How much salt would be left if an entire ocean evaporated?

EXPLORE

Resources of the Paleozoic Era

In the Explore Activity on pages 46–47, you saw that when salt water evaporated, the salt stayed behind. The more salt in the water, the more salt left behind. When people find large salt deposits on Earth, it's a clue that a large body of salt water must have once been in that place.

Most of the evidence of the events that occurred during the Paleozoic Era has either changed or eroded over the course of millions of years since then. Trying to understand the past is like doing detective work.

Paleontologist

Notice that the words *paleontologist* (pā lē ən tol´ ə jist) and *Paleozoic* start in the same way. The words come from a Greek word part that means "long ago." Paleontology is the field of science dealing with fossils.

Paleontologists study fossils to construct their hypotheses of what, when, how, and why different forms of ancient life have existed on Earth as it has changed over time. Paleontologists are the ones who study the dinosaurs, mastodons, woolly mammoths, plants, and other animals of the past.

Paleontologists have to know about geology to study rocks and landforms, and about biology to study forms of life that have existed over time.

Paleontologists work at colleges, in museums, for governments, or in private industry exploring Earth's natural resources.

Paleontologists spend a lot of time outside looking for fossils. Like detectives, these scientists have to examine and think about the clues they have.

Paleontologists also spend a lot of time examining fossils in a laboratory. Scientists develop a logical explanation of what, why, when, and how things happened, based on their often-limited evidence.

The interpretation of evidence makes up history and science, not facts themselves. When new evidence is found or the evidence is looked at in a new way, theories change. If you like mysteries and trying to explain the unknown, paleontology is for you.

Salt Deposits

Throughout the Paleozoic Era, glaciers melted and then developed again as the climate changed from warm to cold. When they melted, shallow seas covered much of the land on Earth. Now, like then, salt in the sea comes from rocks on land that dissolve during erosion and weathering processes. Water evaporates from the oceans but leaves the salt behind.

During some time periods, there were changing landforms and many large barrier reefs made of coral that trapped water from the ocean. When the sea level dropped, the trapped water evaporated. Just as in the Explore Activity on pages 46–47, salt was left behind. Over time, layers of soil and rocks buried this salt. Some of these salt deposits are over 1.5 kilometers (about 1 mile) below the surface of Earth.

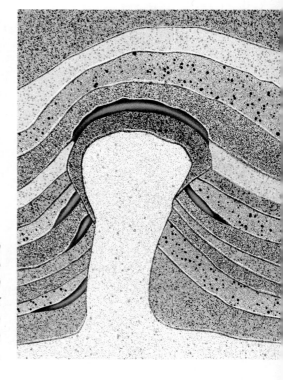

Sometimes we get salt deposits from salt domes laid down during the Paleozoic Era. They are formed when beds of salt flow upward and break through overlying rock. Most of the time salt deposits come from evaporating sea water.

Salt mines are dry and have stayed the same for millions of years. Salt mines are found on every continent on Earth.

Although many deposits formed from the ancient seas during the Paleozoic Era, many others formed during different eras. What does that tell you about oceans?

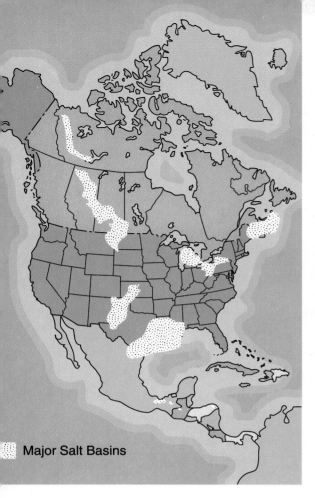

Major Salt Basins

In North America, salt deposits are found in 32 of the United States and Canada. Salt deposits in New York, Utah, Ohio, Kansas, and Ontario formed during the Paleozoic Era. Salt in Louisiana and Texas probably formed during the Mesozoic Era.

Social Studies Link

Salt Deposits in the United States

Find out where the closest salt deposits are to you. Ask your librarian or the U.S. Geological Survey in the phone directory for help. Find out how and when these deposits formed. Then write a description or draw a picture of what the area must have been like when the salt deposits formed. Share your findings with your family and classmates.

TRY THIS Activity!

Properties of Salt

What is it about salt that makes it so valuable to us? How can it stay in salt mines for millions of years?

What You Need
cup, hot water, 1 c salt, 2 containers, spoon, hand lens, *Activity Log* page 24.

Fill the cup half full of hot water and pour the water and 1 c salt into one container. Stir until some dissolves. Pour half of the water solution into the other container. Put 1 container in a cool area and the other container in a warm place. After 2 days, examine each container. Record your observations in your ***Activity Log.***

Take out the salt crystals and examine them carefully with the hand lens. How are the salt crystals in each container the same? How are they different? What temperature conditions allowed the salt to form large crystals? What can you infer about the past that could have encouraged huge salt deposits to form?

The Late Paleozoic Era

Earth processes from the early Paleozoic Era produced the salt used on your crackers and pretzels. Earth's processes from the late Paleozoic Era also produced important resources.

Throughout much of this time, the climate on Earth was much warmer than it is today. Glaciers had melted, and large tropical swamps covered much of North America and Europe. When the trees died, their remains developed into the coal we use for fuel today.

About 400 million years ago, North America collided with Europe. This collision formed the Appalachian Mountains in eastern North America and the Caledonian Mountains in northwestern Europe. These two continents then collided with a third landmass made up of what is now Africa, South America, and Australia, and formed the Ural Mountains in Asia.

About 350 million years ago

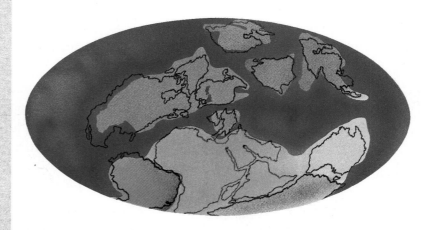

TRY THIS

Activity!

Back to Coal

It's time to check the activity you started at the beginning of this unit.

What You Need
container with sand, rotting leaves, sticks, and ferns, sand, *Activity Log* page 25

Observe what has taken place in the container. Write any changes in your ***Activity Log.*** Put 2 cm sand on top of the rotting matter. Observe and record what happens. Then carefully pour off the water and allow the material to dry. Predict which layer will eventually turn into coal if given enough time. Why do you think coal can be burned for fuel and other rocks cannot?

Coal is a sedimentary rock. Many **sedimentary** (sed´ə men´tə rē) **rocks** are rocks made of loose Earth materials that are cemented or squeezed together by natural processes. Do this activity to make a sedimentary sandwich to see how sedimentary rocks are formed.

TRY THIS

Activity!

A Sedimentary Sandwich

Rocks from peanut butter? See how it can be done.

What You Need
2 slices of bread, fruit spread, peanut butter (crunchy if possible), plastic knife, *Activity Log* page 26

Spread some peanut butter on one slice of bread. Then put fruit spread on top of the peanut butter. Put the second slice of bread on top of the fruit-spread layer. You can then eat your "sedimentary" sandwich.

How is your sandwich like a sedimentary rock formation? If you laid a concrete block on top of your sandwich, what would happen to it over time? Are you developing a type of sedimentary rock in the coal activity? How is it the same as and different from the process of sedimentary rock formation on Earth?

Your "sedimentary" sandwich was a model of sedimentary rock. The bread was cemented together by the peanut butter and fruit spread. Some examples of sedimentary rocks are limestone, sandstone, and coal.

Sandstone

Shell Limestone

Coal

Coal forms in swampy areas when plants decay. It takes about 1–2 meters (3–7 feet) of plant matter to make a bed of coal 0.3 meters (1 foot) thick.

Minds On! What kinds of climate conditions cause swamps to develop? Can you think of any swamps that currently exist? Where are they? Could coal be forming there? ●

This is a coal mine in Australia. Coal can be found on every continent, including Antarctica. The United States, northern Asia, China, Australia, Germany, South Africa, Poland, India, and Great Britain all have coal deposits worth mining.

Stages of Coal Formation

1 **Peat** *(pēt)—rotted plant matter found in bogs and swamps. It is about 75 to 90 percent water and is burned as fuel in many parts of the world.*

2 **Lignite** *(lig′ nīt)— soft brown coal that has lost most of its moisture.*

3 **Bituminous** *(bī tū′ mə nəs)— soft black coal that has lost all its moisture and most other impurities. It produces a smoky yellow flame, ash, and sulfur compounds.*

4 **Anthracite** *(an′ thrə sīt)—coal that is formed due to intense pressure and heat. The last stage of coal is metamorphic rock. It is the cleanest coal to burn.*

Using Coal for Fuel

Coal is burned to heat some homes. On a large scale, however, it is used in addition to oil, gas, and nuclear energy to make electrical energy. Electrical energy not only heats buildings, but it serves a variety of other purposes as well.

Is burning coal worth the pollution it causes and the trouble it takes to mine it? There is a lot of it in the United States, which consumes a huge percentage of the world's energy resources. In addition, unlike oil and gas, people estimate that we will not run out of it for several hundred years. For these reasons and others, people are exploring ways to clean the third stage, high-sulfur coal. But so far the cleaning process is very expensive.

Find out where your local electrical energy comes from. What type of fuel is used to produce it?

Consider the alternatives to the use of coal as fuel for electrical energy. What are the advantages and disadvantages of each fuel? What might some other sources of energy be? Compare each fuel to coal. Talk to your friends and family about your conclusions. Decide if you want to try to change the type of fuel being used to produce your electricity.

Coal-burning power plant

55

Life in the Paleozoic Era

There is no evidence of life on land at the beginning of the Paleozoic Era. However, warm climates and water encouraged the evolution of a large number of marine animals with shells and skeletons. The middle of the Paleozoic Era is known as the "Age of Fish," because there were so many varieties of them during this period.

Throughout the Paleozoic Era, living things spread from the sea across the lands. Changes in climate resulted in the extinction of some of these forms of life. But many have continued through the Mesozoic and into the Cenozoic Era.

Almost three-fourths of the amphibians that adapted to land became extinct. But these extinctions paved the way for reptiles to continue to evolve in the Mesozoic Era.

Eryops

Platysomus

Tristychius

Acanthodes

Sum It Up

We have learned much about Earth's history during the Paleozoic Era by studying the continents' movements, changes in climate, and evolving life. Conditions may not have been as favorable for as many varieties of life-forms to evolve as we have today.

If the climate had not warmed, oceans would not have built the barrier reefs that trapped salt in salt mines. Giant trees would not have developed to form the coal we mine today.

Critical Thinking

1. How was Earth during the Paleozoic Era different from Earth during the Mesozoic and Cenozoic Eras? How was it the same?
2. Do you think people are using up coal faster than it is being formed? What evidence do you have of this?
3. Will we ever use up all of Earth's salt? Why or why not?

By the end of the Paleozoic Era, forests of conifers were beginning to replace swampland ferns and mosses. When the continents merged there were mass extinctions of animals and plants.

Acanthodes

Crassigyrinus

Canobius

Some Things Just Don't Change

The Precambrian
4.6 Billion to 570 Million Years Ago

People have buried time capsules as records of certain times and places. Years later people have dug them up and looked back into the past. Earth's time capsule is in its rocks. Rocks are the only record we have of what happened on Earth over 600 million years ago.

Activity!

What Remains?

Once an organism dies, how long will its parts be preserved? Try this activity to observe changes in plant leaves.

What You Need

small tree branch with leaves, *Activity Log* page 27

Describe your tree branch in your *Activity Log*. Then put your tree branch outside where it will be undisturbed for 1 week. After 1 week, observe it. Which parts have changed? Which haven't?

If you left the branch in the same spot for a year, what would happen to it? What would happen to it after 10 years? After 100 years? After 100 million years? What could you do to preserve your tree branch? Is there anything you could do to preserve it for 600 million years?

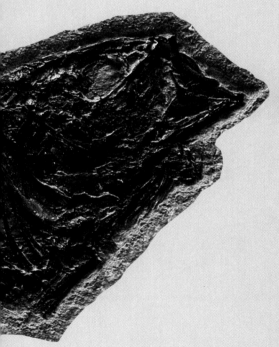

Fish fossil

There are many ways, in addition to burying time capsules, that you can preserve things you want to keep. For example, you can press leaves between the pages of a book. You can put pictures and letters in scrapbooks.

When left alone, matter changes form on Earth. It's seldom preserved. Even rocks change over time. The forces on Earth constantly break things down through weathering, erosion, and decay. It's only by chance that a plant or animal is buried in sediment and preserved. It's only by chance that rocks from long ago remain unchanged. But when that happens, we get a glimpse into the past.

Minds On!
On page 27 in your *Activity Log*, describe how we know about living things in the past that are not frozen or buried in one piece. What clues could we possibly have about the life-forms that existed 600 million years ago? Earth processes destroyed the evidence, but they have also preserved some of it. ●

Activity!

Making a Good Impression

Fossils are what is left of organisms that once lived. Their remains are preserved in several ways. In this activity you'll make your own fossils to discover one way they are preserved.

What You Need

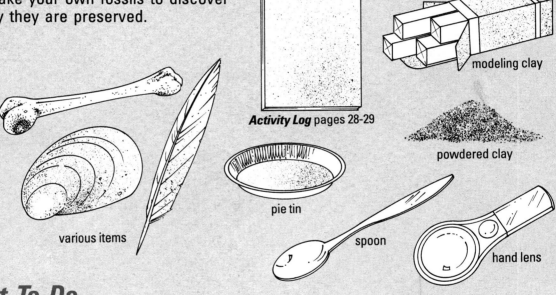

Activity Log pages 28-29

modeling clay

powdered clay

pie tin

spoon

hand lens

various items

What To Do

1 Cover the bottom of the pie tin with a layer of modeling clay about 5 cm thick.

2 Firmly press the various items into the clay, but don't cover the items with clay.

3 Then, carefully remove each item. Examine the imprints in the clay. Use your hand lens to look more closely. Write your observations in your *Activity Log.*

4 Scoop the mixed clay into the pie tin with modeling clay. Pat the clay until it's smooth.

5 Allow the clay to dry in the sun for two days.

6 Remove the clay "fossil" from the clay. Observe what you have and draw a picture of both the impression and the clay "fossil" in your *Activity Log.*

What Happened?

1. If you only looked at the imprints made by others in the class, would you be able to tell what objects made each imprint?

2. Were all the imprints in your class equally good? Why or why not?

What Now?

1. What do you think the modeling clay represents?

2. What does the powdered clay represent?

3. If you looked at the imprints in 10 years, would you be able to identify what object made each imprint? Would you be able to identify them in 100 years?

4. How are your "fossils" different from real ones?

EXPLORE

Fossils

In the Explore Activity on page 60–61, you saw that organisms or parts of organisms could be preserved as imprints. Fossils are the remains or traces of ancient life-forms that have been preserved in the rocks of Earth's sediment.

The Precambrian represents about seven-eighths of Earth's history. It began when Earth first appeared. It lasted until lots of fossils of organisms with hard parts appeared in the fossil record. But we know less about this period than any other era.

This is partly because Precambrian fossils are hard to find. The few organisms that lived had some hard parts that were preserved in the fossil record. And over time, Earth's processes have destroyed much of the evidence.

Trilobite

Molds *are impressions in sediment from the hard parts of organisms. In nature, the parts gradually decay or change form. In the Explore Activity, you removed the parts of the organisms after making the molds in the clay.*

Casts *are the result of filling in molds from which you get an exact impression of an organism. In nature, minerals fill molds and become fossil casts. In the Explore Activity, you made casts of these molds.*

Trace fossils are evidence of the activity of once-living things. The fossils that do exist from the Precambrian are usually trace fossils. The organism itself is completely gone. Dinosaur footprints are trace fossils from the Mesozoic Era. Worm burrows are trace fossils from the Precambrian.

Paleontologists study fossils of ancient life-forms. They use the fossils to draw conclusions about what Earth was like throughout its history. The kinds of organisms that lived show what ancient environments and climates were like.

Literature Link

Dinosaurs Walked Here and Other Stories Fossils Tell

Read Patricia Lauber's book again. In your **Activity Log** on page 30, make a list of all the different organism fossils that are mentioned. Write the ages of the fossils. Group them by the eras in which they lived. Are there any fossils in this book to list from the Precambrian? Why or why not?

Trilobite

Over time, Earth processes can wipe out evidence of fossils. The rocks dated as Precambrian have gone through many, many changes. Rocks have been forming, eroding, and reforming throughout geologic time. Many have been changed because of heat and pressure in Earth's surface.

1

2

Sometimes old rocks and fossils are exposed due to erosion. Rock layers usually reveal the order in which things happened in Earth's history. The youngest fossils are on the top layer and the oldest are on the bottom layers.

3

4

Precambrian layers are the hardest to uncover because they're sometimes below 600 million years of sediment.

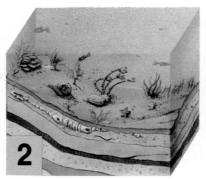

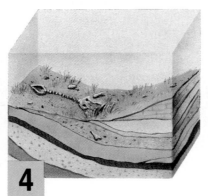

The fossilization of a Plesiosaur, a reptile from the Mesozoic Era.

Arizona's Grand Canyon provides a view of many strata (strā´ tə) or layers of rock spanning the longest geologic history that is exposed on Earth. These strata contain information about 2 billion years of this canyon's geologic history.

The fossil record gives concrete clues about organisms that have lived on Earth. But it also gives clues when no fossils are found. It tells when an organism became extinct. We know that dinosaurs and trilobites became extinct at certain times in the past, because there was no fossil record of them after a particular date. Extinctions are indicated by the disappearance of organisms from the fossil record.

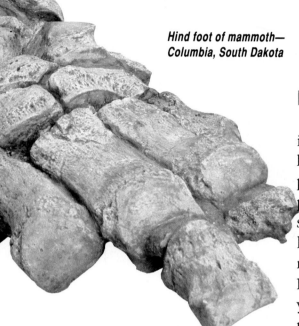

Hind foot of mammoth—Columbia, South Dakota

Finding Fossils

Fossils can be found almost anywhere there is sedimentary rock. To learn about Earth's history, geologists and paleontologists identify places where they think fossils may have been preserved. In other cases, they use techniques such as core sampling and deep-sea drilling to look for records in layers of rocks. In 1986, a miner in the La Toca amber mine in the Dominican Republic found a 40 million-year-old, complete frog fossil that had been preserved in the amber.

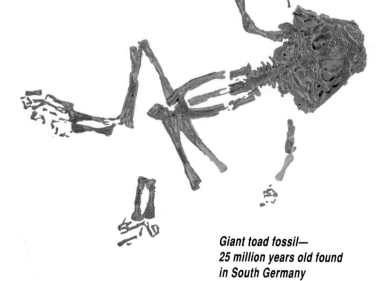

Giant toad fossil—25 million years old found in South Germany

65

Studying Evidence

To learn about the Precambrian, geologists and paleontologists have had to rely on the little evidence they have. They look at the fossil record and rock strata to piece together the puzzle of this period of Earth's history.

Evidence of glaciers has been found in Canada and South Africa dating from Precambrian times. The earliest evidence of glaciers dates back 2.3 billion years.

From this, earth scientists inferred that climate changes occurred throughout the Precambrian to cause ice ages on Earth. Did ice ages occur in all other eras of Earth's history?

Plate Tectonics

Because plate tectonics played such an important role throughout the other eras, we assume the process was at work during the Precambrian as well.

About 2.5 billion years ago, the first continents appeared. The underlying plates were thinner and the boundaries weren't as well defined. But over time, mountains and other evidence of plate boundaries have disappeared. It's difficult to figure out the positions of the Precambrian continents and where the Precambrian plate boundaries were.

Geologists have to use the little evidence that exists to reconstruct the shape of the Precambrian continents.

A project at the Gulf of Bothnia between Finland and Sweden, far from any present boundary of the Eurasian plate, confirms the workings of plate tectonics. It appears that one of these ancient plates slid under another when the two plates collided.

About 670 million years ago

Rocks indicate that the continents formed one giant landmass like Pangaea during this time.

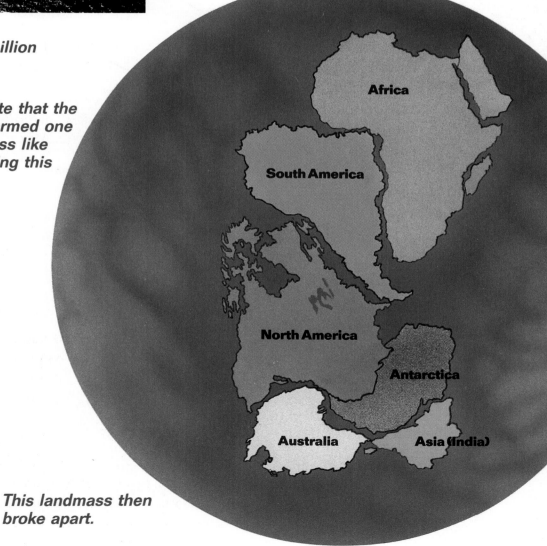

Africa

South America

North America

Antarctica

Australia

Asia (India)

This landmass then broke apart.

Precambrian Minerals and Rocks

Many of the metals we use today appear to have been on Earth from its early days. Precambrian rocks are important sources of almost every kind of mineral resource except fossil fuels. Fossil fuels develop from living things that didn't exist during the Precambrian.

Many Precambrian rocks contain important ore deposits. Ores are rocks or minerals that are mined for profit.

When oxygen combines with iron, it makes iron oxide or rust. When you see rocks with reddish streaks, they usually contain iron that has been exposed to oxygen. This same process may have been responsible for some red bands in iron deposits during the Precambrian. Do the next activity to see how iron and oxygen react.

Nickel

Gold

Iron

Copper

Uranium

Silver

All of these minerals are found in Precambrian rocks.

TRY THIS

Activity!

Safety Tip: Be careful when handling the steel wool. It can give you splinters.

Iron and Oxygen

What happens when oxygen meets iron?

What You Need
steel wool, water, bowl, *Activity Log* page 31

Wet the steel wool with the water and then put it in the bowl. Write a prediction about what will happen in your *Activity Log*. Allow it to sit for 3 days. Record your observations of change. Was your prediction correct?

Diamonds are the hardest minerals on Earth. They're found in rocks in many places in the world, including Australia, Zaire, South Africa, and northern Asia.

Diamonds are pure, hard forms of carbon, the same element coal is made of. Unlike coal, however, they're formed under intense heat and pressure deep underground.

Igneous (ig´ nē əs) **rock** is rock formed when melted rock-like material, rises from Earth's mantle, cools, and hardens. Earth's crust is made largely of igneous rocks—**granite** (gran´ it) on the continents, and **basalt** (bə sôlt´) under the oceans. Both are buried under sedimentary rock.

Evidence suggests that basalt probably formed most of the earliest crust on the continents and under the oceans.

On the continents, granite formed when plate tectonics melted and remelted the basalt.

Some rocks have changed since the Precambrian. Rocks older than 3.7 billion years are hard to find. Examples we do have of Precambrian rocks help us confirm that some things have remained constant throughout Earth's history.

Social Studies Link

Precambrian Time Line

Review the dates discussed in the description of the Precambrian. In your *Activity Log* on page 32, make a time line showing the different events that occurred at each of the dates mentioned. Construct your time line so that you have proportional space between the different time periods.

Life in the Precambrian

People have found fossil impressions of one-celled, bacteria-like, microscopic life-forms in sedimentary rock. They lived in the oceans 3.5 billion years ago, over a billion years after the beginning of Earth. They may have been the first living things on Earth.

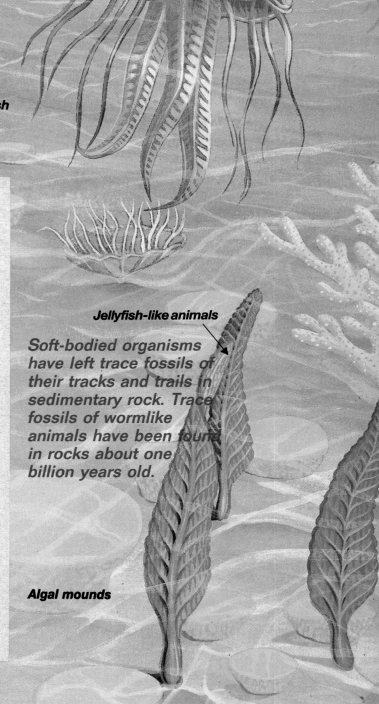

Jellyfish

Jellyfish-like animals

Soft-bodied organisms have left trace fossils of their tracks and trails in sedimentary rock. Trace fossils of wormlike animals have been found in rocks about one billion years old.

Algal mounds

TRY THIS Activity!

Back to Coal Again

It's time to observe what's happening in your fossil-fuel container that you started in the beginning of this unit.

What You Need
container with formations, *Activity Log* page 33

Look into your container. How have things changed since you made your last observations? Record the changes in your *Activity Log*. Remove a sample of the sediment. Look for evidence of the plant life you placed in the container. How has it changed over time? How is it the same as and different from a fossil that may be preserved over time on Earth?

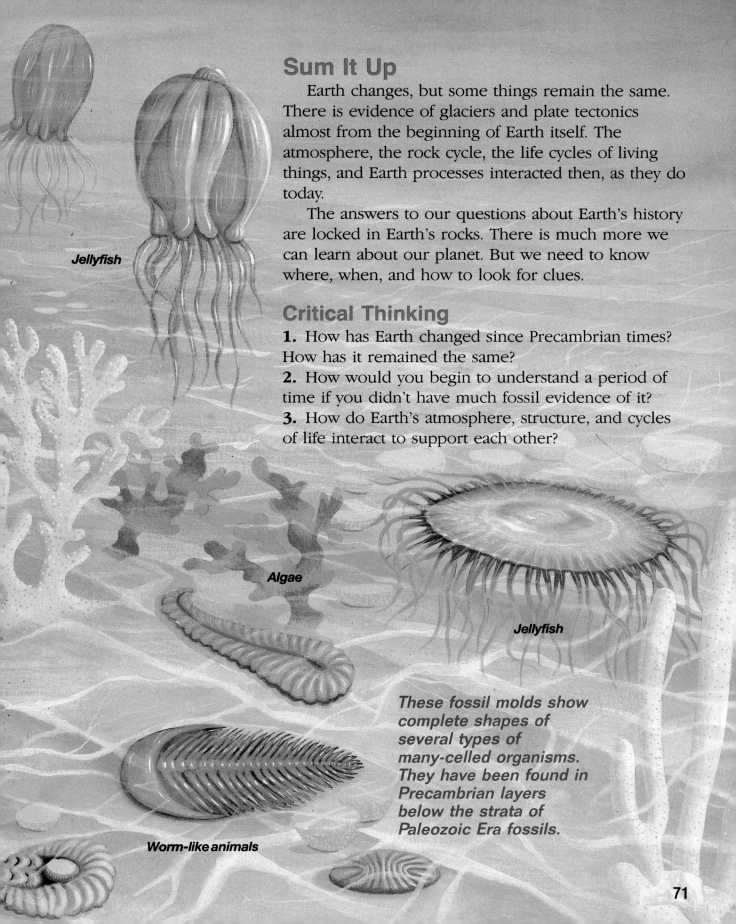

Sum It Up

Earth changes, but some things remain the same. There is evidence of glaciers and plate tectonics almost from the beginning of Earth itself. The atmosphere, the rock cycle, the life cycles of living things, and Earth processes interacted then, as they do today.

The answers to our questions about Earth's history are locked in Earth's rocks. There is much more we can learn about our planet. But we need to know where, when, and how to look for clues.

Critical Thinking

1. How has Earth changed since Precambrian times? How has it remained the same?

2. How would you begin to understand a period of time if you didn't have much fossil evidence of it?

3. How do Earth's atmosphere, structure, and cycles of life interact to support each other?

Jellyfish

Algae

Jellyfish

These fossil molds show complete shapes of several types of many-celled organisms. They have been found in Precambrian layers below the strata of Paleozoic Era fossils.

Worm-like animals

Birth of Earth

The Formation of Earth
4.6 Billion Years Ago

This is the way the world ends
Not with a bang but a whimper.
 T.S. Eliot, 1925

We may not know how the world will end, but people have been thinking, hypothesizing, and theorizing about how it began. However that happened, it involved a lot of energy that gave Earth its structure and allowed it to sustain life.

Earth is big and it's been around for a long time. It's so important to us that it's often hard to imagine that once it didn't exist. When you think of Earth in its place in the rest of the universe, it can seem pretty small. It's only the fifth largest of the nine planets in the solar system.

The sun itself is an average-sized star with a diameter of 1.4 million kilometers (864 thousand miles), 109 times bigger than Earth. The sun contains 99.8 percent of all the matter in our solar system. In the night sky, from Earth, we see only other stars, not their planets. From those stars, you'd see only our sun and not Earth.

Minds On! You know that Earth is about 4.6 billion years old. In this unit, you've looked at Earth's history. How do you think it got its start? Where did it come from? What's it made of? What happened before the Precambrian? Write your ideas in your *Activity Log* on page 34. ●

Looking at the innermost parts of Earth may give us some clues about its birth. You're sitting or standing on Earth's crust. You know that this crust is riding on the mantle layer of softened, hot, rocklike material. But what's at the center of Earth?

Joshua Tree National Monument, California

Activity!

Journey to the Center of Earth

In this activity you'll make a model of Earth to see what the layers are like.

What You Need

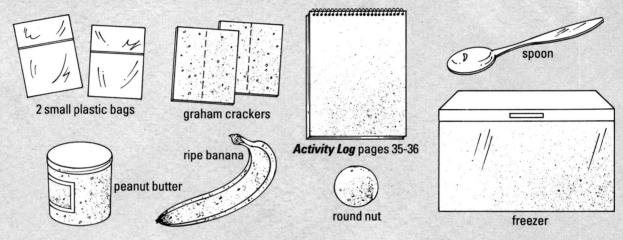

2 small plastic bags

graham crackers

Activity Log pages 35–36

spoon

peanut butter

ripe banana

round nut

freezer

What To Do

1 Wash your hands. Take a spoonful of peanut butter and place a nut in the middle of the peanut butter. Cover the nut with peanut butter. The thickness of the peanut butter should be about as wide as the entire nut.

2 Place the peeled banana into a plastic bag and mash the banana until smooth. Place the covered nut into the bag and cover it with a layer of mashed banana just a bit thicker than the peanut butter.

3 Put graham crackers into another bag to break them up into pieces. Arrange them so that the banana layer is completely covered with graham crackers.

4 Freeze your "Earth," then bite into this model of Earth and draw a picture of its layers. Then you may eat the whole thing.

What Happened?

1. What does the graham cracker represent?
2. What does the banana represent?
3. What do you think the peanut butter and nut represent?

What Now?

1. Unlike your model, you know Earth's outer crust is mainly rock and the mantle is softened, rocklike material. What do you think Earth's core is made of?
2. Where do you think materials in the layers of Earth come from?

EXPLORE

75

The Formation of Earth

In the Explore Activity on pages 74–75, you made a healthful model of Earth. You used different foods to represent its different layers.

Of course, no one has ever dug deep enough into Earth's layers to reach the outer or inner core, or even the mantle. By studying the way the energy from earthquake waves moves through Earth, scientists found out that the inner core was solid and the outer core and much of the mantle were mostly liquid. Like sound waves, ocean waves, or light waves, earthquake waves behave differently when they pass through different types of materials.

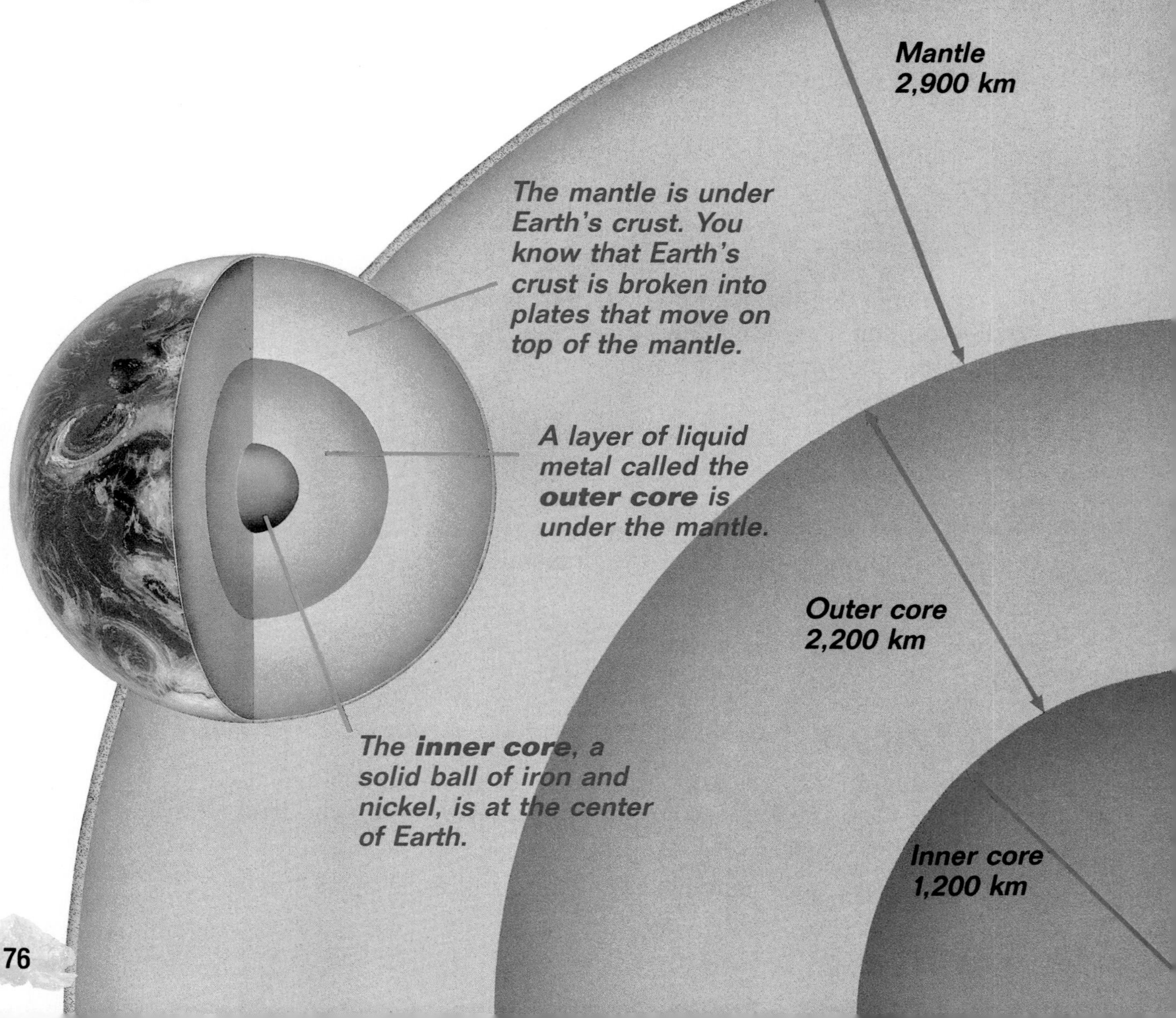

**Crust
35 km**

**Mantle
2,900 km**

The mantle is under Earth's crust. You know that Earth's crust is broken into plates that move on top of the mantle.

A layer of liquid metal called the outer core is under the mantle.

**Outer core
2,200 km**

The inner core, a solid ball of iron and nickel, is at the center of Earth.

**Inner core
1,200 km**

Minds On! Certain types of fruit are often used to show the layers of Earth. Which fruits remind you of the structure of Earth? Make a list of possibilities in your *Activity Log* on page 37. ●

Even though the outer layer of Earth has cooled and hardened forming a crust over the planet, Earth's interior has remained very hot. Molten rock and gases continue to erupt from beneath the surface. What evidence do we have today that the interior of Earth is hot?

Lighter materials rose to form the outer core and mantle.

Even lighter materials formed the thin outer crust.

The lightest materials formed an outer layer of gases.

Scientists theorize that Earth formed from a spinning cloud of dust and gases in space. Gravity pulled the more dense iron and nickel inward to form the inner core.

Even though we think rocks on the surface of Earth are heavy, the materials in the inner core are much more dense.

Eventually the gases developed into Earth's atmosphere. At first it was a hot, steamy mixture of gases. Volcanic eruptions from Earth gave off lots of steam as they do today.

When the steam from the eruptions condensed in the atmosphere, it fell as rain. Before Earth cooled, the water turned back into steam. When the crust cooled enough for this rainwater to collect on the surface, Earth's oceans were born.

Today Earth's atmosphere, as part of the water cycle, still holds much water. If it all fell as rain, it would cover the entire surface of Earth with 2.5 centimeters (about 1 inch) of rain.

Earth's atmosphere has layers. The highest of these layers reaches hundreds of kilometers above Earth's surface. Like a blanket, these layers hold in the sun's heat. At the same time, the atmosphere protects life on Earth from the sun's harmful ultraviolet rays. The oxygen in it is responsible for protecting life from the ultraviolet rays. Remember that oxygen entered the atmosphere during the Precambrian when early life-forms first evolved.

To some extent, the atmosphere also protects Earth from some small objects in space that could collide with it, like asteroids and meteorites. As these objects travel through the atmosphere, most burn up from the friction caused by moving rapidly through the atmosphere's matter.

Some objects do get through, however. There is evidence of impacts on Earth from various time periods, including the present. One hypothesis is that the impact of an asteroid caused the extinction of the dinosaurs at the end of the Mesozoic Era.

In contrast, the moon has no atmosphere or weather to protect it or cover up signs of these objects from space. The moon's craters are evidence of many hits.

In 1991, a fist-sized meteorite fell in front of a 13-year-old boy standing in his front yard north of Indianapolis, Indiana. It was still warm when he picked it up.

Theories About the Birth of Earth

Now that you've taken a bite out of "Earth's layers," think about where the materials came from. People have developed many hypotheses and theories about the origin of Earth. Think about the following theories about our solar system's birth. Which theory do you think is correct? Why? Base your decision on what you know about the Earth's structure and history.

Tidal Theory

According to the tidal theory, the gravity of a passing star pulled part of the sun's matter away. This matter then split into parts that condensed and became the planets we know today.

Minds On! What types of models can you think of that fit the tidal theory? How is it like the breakup of Pangaea? How is it different? How is it like a mother and her offspring? Discuss your ideas with your classmates. ●

Nebular Hypothesis

In this explanation, gravity is said to have caused a spinning, shrinking cloud of gas and dust, called a **nebula** (neb´ yə le´), to produce our star, the sun. This cloud threw off pieces that condensed to form planets and their moons. Gravity is the force that caused the sun and planets to form. It's also the force that created and maintains the orbits of the planets and moons.

TRY THIS

Activity!

My Little Nebula

What would a nebula be like?

What You Need
cup, water, pencil shavings, spoon, *Activity Log* page 38

Drop some pencil shavings into the water. Use your spoon to stir the water in a circular motion. Observe what happens to the shavings. Write your observations in your *Activity Log*. What was at the center of the rotation? Did all the pencil shavings go to the center of the rotation? How is this like the motion described in the nebular hypothesis? How is it different?

Exploding Supernova

*In this hypothesis our sun had a sister star called a supernova. A **supernova** (sü ́ pər nō ́ və) is a star that suddenly increases in light and then fades.*

This sister star exploded. The pieces of debris created by the explosion formed the planets.

Accretion (ə krē´ shən) is the process of growth by the slow increase of particles. Like snowflakes that collide and stick together to form clusters, the accretion theory says that a cold cloud of gases collided and then shrank. The contraction formed a star, our sun, at its center. Other condensing masses of gas and dust formed the planets.

Minds On! What do you know of that shrinks? What causes shrinkage? What do you think could cause a cloud of gas to shrink? ●

Language Arts Link

Time To Choose

Compare your own hypothesis about the formation of Earth with these four ideas. Which do you think is the most logical? In your **Activity Log** on page 39, make a list of questions you have about each of these ideas. Go to the library to look for answers. Record what you find. Then decide which idea makes the most sense to you. Write a persuasive argument about why you think the idea you chose is correct. Be ready to defend your position.

Earth is one of nine planets in our solar system. The sun is the source of almost all energy on Earth. It provides the energy for plants to photosynthesize and provide food and oxygen for other living things. It's the source of energy that creates the water and rock cycles. But in terms of the universe, it's only one of 100 billion stars that make up one cluster of stars in the universe.

How long the universe has existed and how long it'll exist are questions that occupy the minds of many brilliant scientists, philosophers, artists, and students like yourself.

*The origin of the universe is a much bigger question than the origin of our sun and Earth. The **Big Bang Theory** is currently the most accepted theory of the origin of the universe.*

In simple terms, it states that a massive explosion occurred that marked the beginning of the universe and started its expansion.

Somewhere else in the universe, other life may very well exist. At present the only life we know of is right here on Earth. But there is no evidence of life on Earth the first billion years of its existence. If life evolved here, it could have evolved elsewhere.

Extraterrestrial Life

Many science-fiction books deal with the possibility of **extraterrestrial** (ek´ strə tə res´ trē əl) life. Extraterrestrial life refers to life outside our solar system. Madeleine L'Engle's *A Wrinkle in Time*, Gene Roddenberry's *Star Trek* series, John Christopher's *The City of Gold and Lead*, and others have extraterrestrial characters. Read one of these books. Look for descriptions of extraterrestrial life. In your ***Activity Log*** on page 40, compare and contrast them to the life-forms that evolved on Earth throughout geologic time.

Sum It Up

Whatever the cause of Earth's formation, a great deal of energy was involved. Energy causes change in matter. Energy changes water from the oceans to a gas in the air, and to a solid in glaciers. Energy moves matter within Earth's mantle that causes mountains to form. Energy causes wind to erode rocks and sculpt them into new shapes.

We may never know where the energy present within Earth came from. But we can appreciate its effects. Because of this energy, Earth is a changing planet that has the ability to sustain life. Do you think energy helps sustain life on other planets?

Critical Thinking

1. What are the similarities between the theories about the formation of Earth? What are the major differences?

2. What information about Earth's structure would be helpful in trying to understand the formation of Earth?

3. Why do people care about learning how Earth formed? Should they?

It's About Time

It's easy to think that Earth belongs to humans. People are adapted to live almost anywhere on the planet. We have changed it more than any other animal we know of.

We have also caused the extinction or near extinction of many other living things through our changes on Earth. We might even begin to think that we control Earth. But do we really?

Earth has been here a lot longer than we have. Other living things have been here much longer than we have. There have been mass extinctions of plants and animals long before humans were on the planet.

Plate tectonics has caused the continents to come together and move apart, not once but several times throughout geologic time. Mountains have grown up and worn down through plate tectonics and erosion. Oceans have risen and fallen.

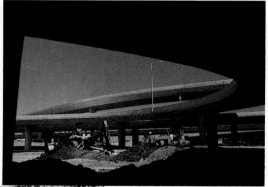

We have built roads, created lakes, blown up mountains and islands. We have farmed the land, developed plants, and tamed animals.

Have you ever asked your parents or grandparents about the "olden days?" When you are 10 or 11 years old, 20 years seems like a long time ago.

When you study United States history, the Civil War and the signing of the Declaration of Independence seem like ages ago. The ancient Mayan, Chinese, and African civilizations are even harder to visualize. So much has happened to humans.

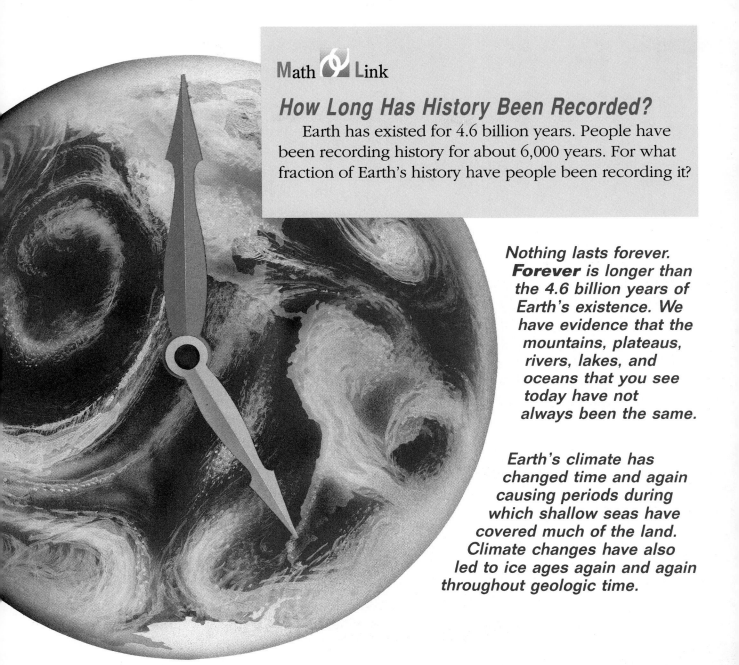

Math ✺ Link

How Long Has History Been Recorded?

Earth has existed for 4.6 billion years. People have been recording history for about 6,000 years. For what fraction of Earth's history have people been recording it?

*Nothing lasts forever. **Forever** is longer than the 4.6 billion years of Earth's existence. We have evidence that the mountains, plateaus, rivers, lakes, and oceans that you see today have not always been the same.*

Earth's climate has changed time and again causing periods during which shallow seas have covered much of the land. Climate changes have also led to ice ages again and again throughout geologic time.

Minds On! Think about what you've just learned about the evolution of Earth's landmasses and organisms. In your *Activity Log* on page 41, describe how different the United States and the organisms that live there would be if plate tectonics never happened. ●

Activity!

It's High Time!

Make a model of a period of geologic time.

What You Need

shoe box, various construction materials, crayons, reference books, *Activity Log* page 42

Choose part of an era of geologic time. Use the reference books to find out more about the climate, the way the continents were arranged, the landforms, and the living things that were on Earth at that time. Then make a diorama or shoe box setting of a scene from that period. Be ready to share it with your classmates.

Time and Earth processes have given us many of the resources that we use today. It's alarming to think that oil, gas, and coal deposits that took millions of years to develop could be used up in just 100 years. We share Earth and its history with all living things. We are all bound together by Earth and by what happens to it.

Geologic time is not over. We can assume that the processes that have shaped Earth will continue to shape it. Are we heading into another ice age? Where will Earth's plates move? What fossil evidence of our lives will we leave on Earth? What do you think will happen in the next million years? Is there anything humans can do to prepare for it?

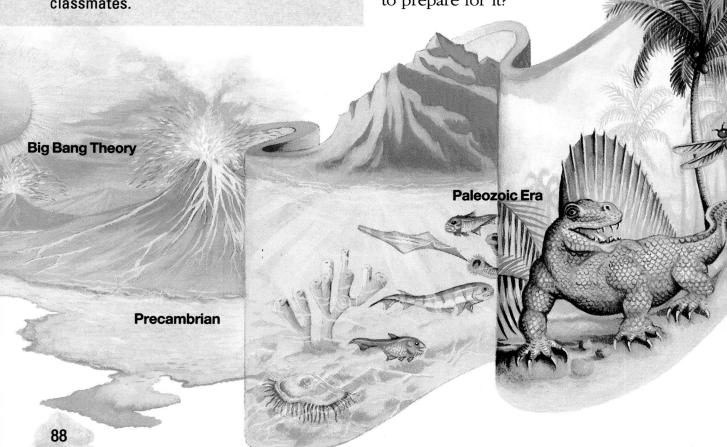

Big Bang Theory

Precambrian

Paleozoic Era

Mesozoic Era

Cenozoic Era

Music/Art Link

Future Earth

In your ***Activity Log*** on page 43, draw a representation of Earth in 100 million years. You may choose to show how Earth's plates will be arranged. You may wish to show the types of organisms that will be on Earth. You may wish to show the types of environments that will be on Earth.

The more you learn about Earth, the better able you will be to answer questions about its past and future. In geologic time, people have only just begun to explore Earth. There is much to learn. Further exploration begins with you and your observations.

GLOSSARY

Use the pronunication key below to help you decode, or read, the pronunciations.

Pronunciation Key

a	at, bad	d	dear, soda, bad
ā	ape, pain, day, break	f	five, defend, leaf, off, cough, elephant
ä	father, car, heart	g	game, ago, fog, egg
âr	care, pair, bear, their, where	h	hat, ahead
e	end, pet, said, heaven, friend	hw	white, whether, which
ē	equal, me, feet, team, piece, key	j	joke, enjoy, gem, page, edge
i	it, big, English, hymn	k	kite, bakery, seek, tack, cat
ī	ice, fine, lie, my	l	lid, sailor, feel, ball, allow
îr	ear, deer, here, pierce	m	man, family, dream
o	odd, hot, watch	n	not, final, pan, knife
ō	old, oat, toe, low	ng	long, singer, pink
ô	coffee, all, taught, law, fought	p	pail, repair, soap, happy
ôr	order, fork, horse, story, pour	r	ride, parent, wear, more, marry
oi	oil, toy	s	sit, aside, pets, cent, pass
ou	out, now	sh	shoe, washer, fish mission, nation
u	up, mud, love, double	t	tag, pretend, fat, button, dressed
ū	use, mule, cue, feud, few	th	thin, panther, both
ü	rule, true, food	th	this, mother, smooth
u̇	put, wood, should	v	very, favor, wave
ûr	burn, hurry, term, bird, word, courage	w	wet, weather, reward
ə	about, taken, pencil, lemon, circus	y	yes, onion
b	bat, above, job	z	zoo, lazy, jazz, rose, dogs, houses
ch	chin, such, match	zh	vision, treasure, seizure

accretion theory (ə krē′ shən)   a theory about the formation of stars, our sun and the planets in which a cold cloud of gases collided and then shrank, forming stars and our sun. Other condensing masses of gas and dust formed the planets.

anthracite (an′ thrə sīt′) the final stage in coal formation; a very hard, glossy black coal with a high carbon content that burns with a low, smokeless flame.

basalt (bə sôlt′)   a dark igneous rock formed at Earth's surface that makes up Earth's crust under the oceans.

Big Bang Theory   a theory stating that the universe originated from the explosion of a dense mass of matter that cooled, collected into clouds, and formed millions of galaxies and stars.

bituminous (bī tü′ mə nəs)   the third stage in coal formation; a soft black coal that burns with a smoky flame.

cast   a fossil formed when minerals fill a fossil mold.

Cenozoic Era (sē′nə zō′ik)   an era of geologic time that began about 65 million years ago and extends to the present.

continental drift   the hypothesis that for millions of years the continents have been slowly moving across Earth's surface and changing their positions.

continental glacier (kon′ tə nen′ təl glā′ shər) a large, flat, dome-shaped ice sheet that moves out from the center in many directions due to pressure from overlying ice and snow; icecap.

crust the outermost layer of Earth that varies in thickness from about 8–35 kilometers (about 5–21 miles).

erosion (i rō′ zhən) the process that happens when glaciers, running water, waves, or wind carry away the soil and rock on Earth's surface.

erratic (i rat′ ik) a rock that is moved from its original place and carried off by a glacier and later deposited.

extinction (ek stingk′ shən) no longer in existence; the end of a plant or animal species.

extraterrestrial (ek′ strə tə res′ trē əl) anything that comes from regions outside Earth and its atmosphere.

fossil (fos′əl) a part or a trace of an organism of a once–living thing preserved in rock.

geologic era (jē′ ə loj′ ik) one of several periods in geologic history.

geologic time scale (jē′ ə loj′ ik) the sequence of events of Earth's history arranged in the order in which they happened.

geologist (jē ol′ ə jist) a scientist who studies the processes that form and change Earth.

geology (jē ol′ ə jē) the science that deals with Earth's structure, composition, and history; this includes the changes that have happened on Earth's surface, and the ways such changes have happened.

glacier (glā′ shər) a large mass of ice moving slowly over Earth's surface; a glacier is formed over a long period of time in areas where the amount of snow that falls in winter is greater than the amount that melts in summer.

granite (gran′it) a light-colored igneous rock formed beneath Earth's surface that makes up most of Earth's continents.

ice age any period of time when glaciers covered much of Earth's surface.

iceberg a large mass of floating ice that has broken off from a glacier or polar icecap.

igneous rock (ig′ nē əs) rock formed from molten Earth material, such as granite and basalt.

imprint to make or produce by pressing a print into a soft sediment.

inner core the solid ball of iron and nickel at the center of Earth.

landform a feature on the surface of Earth, such as a valley, mountain range, plain, or plateau.

lignite (lig′ nīt) the second stage in coal formation; a brownish black, low-quality coal in which layered texture can be seen.

mantle (man′ təl) the middle layer of Earth located between the crust and the outer core.

Mesozoic Era (mez′ ə zō′ ik) a major geologic era that covered the time period from about 250 to 65 million years ago; the age of reptiles.

metamorphic rock (met′ ə môr′ fik) rocks that form from preexisting rocks as the result of temperature and pressure changes.

meteorite (mē′ tē ə rīt′) matter from space that enters the atmosphere and falls to Earth.

mineral (min′ ər əl) a natural, nonliving solid with a specific chemical composition and physical form.

mold a cavity or impression left by an organism in sediment.

moraine (mə rān′) a mass of rock deposited by a melting glacier.

nebula (neb′ yə lə) a bright, cloud-like mass, composed of stars or of dust and gases, visible in the night sky.

ore (ôr) a rock or mineral in Earth containing enough of a metal or useful mineral to make mining profitable.

outer core the layer of liquid metal between Earth's mantle and the inner core.

paleontologist (pā′ lē ən tol ə jist) a scientist who studies fossils.

Paleozoic Era (pā′ lē ə zō′ ik) a major geologic era that covered that time period from about 570 to 250 million years ago.

Pangaea (pan je′ ə) a continent thought to exist during the Mesozoic Era that included most of Earth's present-day continents.

peat (pēt) rotted plant matter found in wet, swampy areas; the first stage in coal formation.

plate tectonics (tek ton′ iks) the theory that Earth's crust is made up of individual plates, some with continents, that slowly move in various directions because of internal forces in the outer mantle.

plates moving rigid blocks of Earth's crust and upper mantle.

Precambrian (prē kam′ brē ən) the time between Earth's formation 4.6 billion years ago and the beginning of the Paleozoic Era.

sedimentary rock (sed′ ə men′ tə rē) rocks formed from the accumulation of separate particles, such as sediments eroded from other rocks and then cemented or squeezed together.

strata (strā′ tə) a layer of material, such as rock or soil, especially one having several layers placed or lying one on top of the other.

supernova (sü′ pər nō′ və) the explosion of a star in which the center collapses under gravity, the outer layers are blown off at high speeds, and the brightness increases greatly before fading.

theory (thē′ ə rē) an explanation or hypothesis supported by facts.

tidal theory a theory about the formation of the planets; gravity of passing star pulled part of the sun's matter away which split it into parts that condensed and became the planets we know today.

trace fossil fossils of the evidence of once living organisms; includes tracks and burrows.

trilobite (trī′ lə bīt′) an extinct sea animal that lived during the Paleozoic Era.

valley glacier (glā′ shər) a glacier that forms in mountain valleys where snow remains year-round.

INDEX

CREDITS

Photo Credits:

Cover, Earth Scenes/E.R. Degginger; **1,** Tony Stone Worldwide/Chicago Ltd; **2-3;** Camerique; **3,** (t) Platinum Studios/1991; **6-7,** Schmist/FPG International; **8-9,** Tony Stone Worldwide/Chicago, Ltd.; **8,** (bl) Stephen J. Krasemann/Peter Arnold, Inc., (bc) Guy Marche/FPG International, (br) Malcolm S. Kirk/Peter Arnold, Inc.; **9,** (bl) Comstock, Inc., (br) Seattle Museum of History & Industry; **12,** (tl) Superstock, (br) ©Platinum Studios; **13,** Kenneth Garret/FPG International, (i) ©Richard Monastersky; **14-15,** Superstock (i) ©Studiohio; **16-17,** Eugen Gebhardt/FPG International; **18-19,** ©Platinum Studio; **21,** (t) E.R. Degginger; **23,** (t) Tom Bean/ALLSTOCK; **24,** ©F. Lisa Beebe/DPI; **25,** (tl) Telegraph Library/FPG International, (br) Bob Waterman/Westlight; **26,** (tr) Thomas Mes/The Stock Market, (bl) Bill Ross/Westlight; **27,** (tl) ©Richard Monastersky, (bl) Grant Heilman Photography, Inc.; **28,** Soufoto/Eastfoto; **30-31,** Comstock, Inc.; **30,** (itl) ©Brent Jones Photography, (itr) Larry Lee/Westlight, (ibl) Superstock, (ibr) Anna Zuckerman/Photoedit; **31,** (tl) Superstock, (tr) The Image Bank/John Callanan, (bl) Tony Freeman/Photoedit; **32-33,** ©K.S. Studio; **41,** (tl) ©Camerique, (br) The Image Bank; **44-45,** The Image Bank/Don Landwehrle; **46-47,** ©Platinum Studios; **48-49,** ©Brent Turner/BLT Productions/1991; **50,** (bl) Comstock, Inc.; **53,** (tr) E.R. Degginger, (bl) ©Camerique, (c,br) Comstock, Inc.; **54,** (bl) Earth Scenes/Breck P. Kent; **55,** (tl) Nikola Zurek/FPG International, (br) E. Alan McGee/FPG International; **58,** (c) The Image Bank/Stephen Mark; **60-61,** ©Platinum Studios; **62,** (c) The Image Bank/Peter Frey; **63,** (tl) Grant Heilman Photography,Inc.; **64,** (tl) Runk/Schoenberger, Grant Heilman, Photography, (br) Lois Frank/Westlight; **65,** (tl) E.R. Degginger/H. Armstrong Roberts, Inc., (br) Runk/Schoenberger/Grant Heilman Photography, Inc.; **66,** (c) Andras Dancs/Tony Stone Worldwide/Chicago, Ltd.; **67,** (tl) ©Buddy Mays; **68,** (tl) Robert Frerck/Tony Stone Worldwide/Chicago, Ltd., (tc) Earth Scenes/E.R. Degginger, (tr) ©John Cancolosi/Peter Arnold, Inc., (cl) Earth Scenes/E.R. Degginger, (cr) ©F&A Michler/Peter Arnold, Inc., (bl) The Image Bank/C. Kuhn, (br) Runk/Schoenberger/Grant Heilman Photography, Inc.; **69,** (tl) ©UNIPHOTO, (cl, cr) Barry L. Runk/Grant Heilman Photography, Inc.; **72-73,** Kathleen Campbell/ALLSTOCK; **74-75,** ©Platinum Studio; **78,** ©Camerique; **79,** ©Greg Montgomery; **86,** (bl) Bruce Coleman, Inc./Hans Reinhard, (br) Mason Morfit/FPG International.

Illustration Credits:

9, Jim Theodore; **10,11, 80, 81, 82, 83, 84, 85,** Greg Harris; **18, 32, 46, 60, 74,** Bob Giuliani; **20 (m), 22, 23, 40,** Stephanie Pershing; **20 (b), 21, 62, 63,** Anne Rhodes; **28, 29, 42, 43, 56, 57, 70, 71, 88, 89,** Holly Jones; **30, 31, 50,** John Edwards; **34, 35, 36, 37, 52, 67,** David Reed; **38, 39, 76, 77, 86, 87,** Henry Hill; **51,** Thomas Kennedy; **54, 64,** Bill Singleton